Higher
Maths

PAST PAPER SOLUTIONS
2009/10 Edition

Steven O'Hagan

George Kinnear

 Higher Still Notes

ISBN: 978 0 9557067 2 1

Published by Higher Still Notes
www.hsn.uk.net

Copyright © Higher Still Notes, 2009

Note: The contents of this book have not been checked or approved by the Scottish Qualifications Authority. They reflect the authors' opinion of good answers to exam questions, and where possible have been checked against publicly available marking instructions.

Printed by Bell & Bain Ltd., Glasgow, Scotland, UK.

Contents

Introduction

How to use this book

Past papers are probably the best practice you can get for the actual exam, so you should plan to do as many as possible. Make sure you practice doing a whole paper in the allocated time, so you can get used to the pace.

The best way to use this book is for checking your answers *after* you have tried the questions yourself. Don't just read the solutions whenever you get stuck!

Here are some features of the book which should help you:

Questions and parts

The question number is shown in the big circle, making it easy to spot at a glance.

All the parts of the question, including subparts, are also labelled.

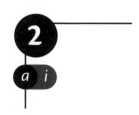

References to notes

The grey box at the start of each solution has pointers to useful sections of our free Higher Maths notes (see below for details).

*See **Integration** §3*

The "§" symbol just means "section", so the example to the right says you should look up Section 3 in the notes for Integration.

Clouds

You'll notice these in a lot of solutions.

They usually contain helpful reminders, or explanations of the steps in the working.

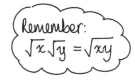

Remember:
$\sqrt{x}\sqrt{y} = \sqrt{xy}$

Get more help with Higher Maths

You can download a free set of Higher Maths notes on our website:

www.hsn.uk.net/Higher-Maths

and you can also join our online forum, where you can chat with other students and ask about any questions you're stuck on:

www.hsn.uk.net/forum

	2006 P1	2006 P2	2007 P1	2007 P2	SQP 1 P1	SQP 1 P2	SQP 2 P1	SQP 2 P2	2008 P1	2008 P2	2009 P1	2009 P2
Straight Lines	1	1	1			1	1, 3, 11		7	1	3, 5, 15, 21	
Functions and Graphs	3	7	3	4a	2, 6, 17		14		8, 17, 19, 20, 23a	3a	10, 14, 23	2a, 5a
Differentiation		3a, 12	9	5a, 6	1, 22	4a, 5b	12, 21	3, 5, 7	21a,c, 22	6	4, 8, 20	1, 2b
Sequences	4		7		5, 21		2, 8		1, 4		1, 6	
Polynomials and Quadratics	8, 9b,c	2, 3b	4, 8a,b	5b, 10a	7, 12, 14, 23		4, 5, 7, 17	2	10, 13, 16, 21b		12, 19	3a
Integration	6	5	8c	10b	3, 13	5a	20, 25	9		7	16	5c
Trigonometry	7	8	6	2, 4b	8, 9, 24	7	9, 23, 24		6, 9	5	7, 11, 24	5b
Circles	2	4	5	3, 5c	10, 15	4b		6	2, 5	4	2, 9	4
Vectors	9a,d	6	2	1	4, 11, 18	2, 4c	10, 15, 16	1	3, 11, 12, 18	2	17, 22	7
Further Calculus	5	9, 10b	10	7	16		6, 18, 19		14, 15	3c	18	
Exponentials and Logarithms	10	11		8, 9, 11	19, 20	6	13, 22	8	23b		10	3b, 6
Wave Functions		10a	11			3		4		3b	13	

Formulae List

Circle

The equation $x^2 + y^2 + 2gx + 2fy + c = 0$ represents a circle centre $(-g, -f)$ and radius $\sqrt{g^2 + f^2 - c}$.

The equation $(x - a)^2 + (y - b)^2 = r^2$ represents a circle centre (a, b) and radius r.

Scalar Product

$\mathbf{a}.\mathbf{b} = |\mathbf{a}||\mathbf{b}|\cos\theta$ where θ is the angle between $\mathbf{a}$ and $\mathbf{b}$.

or $\quad \mathbf{a}.\mathbf{b} = a_1 b_1 + a_2 b_2 + a_3 b_3$ where $\mathbf{a} = \begin{pmatrix} a_1 \\ a_2 \\ a_3 \end{pmatrix}$ and $\mathbf{b} = \begin{pmatrix} b_1 \\ b_2 \\ b_3 \end{pmatrix}$.

Trigonometric formulae

$$\sin(A \pm B) = \sin A \cos B \pm \cos A \sin B$$
$$\cos(A \pm B) = \cos A \cos B \mp \sin A \sin B$$
$$\sin 2A = 2 \sin A \cos A$$
$$\cos 2A = \cos^2 A - \sin^2 A$$
$$= 2\cos^2 A - 1$$
$$= 1 - 2\sin^2 A$$

Table of standard derivatives

$f(x)$	$f'(x)$
$\sin ax$	$a\cos ax$
$\cos ax$	$-a\sin ax$

Table of standard integrals

$f(x)$	$\int f(x)\, dx$
$\sin ax$	$-\dfrac{1}{a}\cos ax + c$
$\cos ax$	$\dfrac{1}{a}\sin ax + c$

1

See **Straight Lines** – (a) §7, (b) §8, (c) §10

a $D = \text{midpoint}_{AC} = \left(\dfrac{-1+7}{2}, \dfrac{12-2}{2} \right) = (3, 5).$

$m_{BD} = \dfrac{5-(-5)}{3-(-2)} = \dfrac{10}{5} = 2.$

So the equation is $y - 5 = 2(x - 3)$

$$y - 5 = 2x - 6$$

$$2x - y - 1 = 0.$$

b $m_{BC} = \dfrac{-2-(-5)}{7-(-2)} = \dfrac{3}{9} = \dfrac{1}{3}.$ So $m_{AE} = -3$ since $AE \perp BC.$

The equation is $y - 12 = -3(x - (-1))$

$$y - 12 = -3x - 3$$

$$3x + y - 9 = 0.$$

c   Solve simultaneously...

$$2x - y = 1 \quad \text{——} \quad ①$$

$$3x + y = 9 \quad \text{——} \quad ②$$

$① + ②: \quad 5x = 10$

$$x = 2.$$

When $x = 2$, $y = 2 \times 2 - 1 = 3$ (using ①).

So the point of intersection is $(2, 3).$

2

(a) See **Circles** §1
(b) See **Circles** §6 and **Straight Lines** §2

$\text{Radius}^2 = CP^2 = \left(1 - (-2)\right)^2 + (6 - 3)^2 = 9 + 9 = 18.$

The equation of the circle is

$(x + 2)^2 + (y - 3)^2 = 18.$

The circle with centre (a, b) and radius r has equation:
$(x-a)^2 + (y-b)^2 = r^2.$

$m_{CP} = \dfrac{6-3}{1-(-2)} = \dfrac{3}{3} = 1.$

So $m_{tgt.} = -1$ since the radius and tangent are perpendicular.

Let Q be the point (x, y). Since C is the midpoint of QP

$$(-2, 3) = \left(\frac{x+1}{2}, \frac{y+6}{2}\right)$$

i.e.

$\dfrac{x+1}{2} = -2 \quad \text{and} \quad \dfrac{y+6}{2} = 3$

$x + 1 = -4 \qquad\qquad y + 6 = 6$

$x = -5 \qquad\qquad\quad y = 0.$

So Q is the point $(-5, 0)$.

The equation of the tangent is

$y - 0 = -1\left(x - (-5)\right)$

$y = -x - 5$

$x + y + 5 = 0.$

3

(a) See **Functions and Graphs** §3
(b) See **Polynomials and Quadratics** §3

i $f(g(x)) = f(2x - 3) = 2(2x - 3) + 3 = 4x - 6 + 3 = 4x - 3$

ii $g(f(x)) = g(2x + 3) = 2(2x + 3) - 3 = 4x + 6 - 3 = 4x + 3.$

$f(g(x)) \times g(f(x)) = (4x - 3)(4x + 3) = 16x^2 - 9$

The least possible value occurs when $x = 0$, so this value is -9.

4

See **Sequences** §4

a) $-1 < 0.8 < 1$

b) **Method 1** $\quad l = \dfrac{b}{1-a}$ where $a = 0.8$ and $b = 12$.

$$l = \frac{12}{1-0.8} = \frac{12}{0.2} = \frac{120}{2} = 60.$$

Method 2 $\quad$ As $n \to \infty$, $u_{n+1} = u_n = l$.

$$l = 0.8l + 12$$
$$0.2l = 12$$
$$l = \frac{12}{0.2}$$
$$= 60.$$

5

See **Differentiation** §8 and **Further Calculus** §4

Stationary points exist where $f'(x) = 0$.

$$f'(x) = 5(2x-1)^4 \times 2 = 10(2x-1)^4 \quad \text{(Remember the Chain Rule)}$$

So $\quad 10(2x-1)^4 = 0$
$$(2x-1)^4 = 0$$
$$2x - 1 = 0$$
$$x = \frac{1}{2}.$$

When $x = \frac{1}{2}$, $y = f\left(\frac{1}{2}\right) = (1-1)^5 = 0$.

So the stationary point is $\left(\frac{1}{2}, 0\right)$.

Nature:

x	$\frac{1}{2}^-$	$\frac{1}{2}$	$\frac{1}{2}^+$
$f'(x)$	$+$	0	$+$
Sketch	$\diagup$	$-$	$\diagup$

So $\left(\frac{1}{2}, 0\right)$ is a rising point of inflection.

6

See **Integration** §5

a The area S is

$$\int_0^1 (x^3 - 6x^2 + 4x + 1)\, dx = \left[\tfrac{1}{4}x^4 - 2x^3 + 2x^2 + x\right]_0^1$$

$$= \tfrac{1}{4} - 2 + 2 + 1$$

$$= \tfrac{5}{4} \text{ square units.}$$

b The second area is

$$-\int_1^2 (x^3 - 6x^2 + 4x + 1)\, dx = -\left[\tfrac{1}{4}x^4 - 2x^3 + 2x^2 + x\right]_1^2$$

> Since the area is below the x-axis.

$$= -\left(\tfrac{16}{4} - 16 + 8 + 2 - \tfrac{5}{4}\right)$$

> from part (a)

$$= -4 + 6 + \tfrac{5}{4}$$

$$= \tfrac{13}{4} \text{ square units.}$$

So the total shaded area is $\tfrac{13}{4} + \tfrac{5}{4} = \tfrac{18}{4} = \tfrac{9}{2}$ square units.

7

See **Trigonometry** §5

$$\sin x° - \sin 2x° = 0$$

$$\sin x° - 2\sin x° \cos x° = 0$$

$$\sin x° (1 - 2\cos x°) = 0$$

> Using:
> $\sin 2A = 2\sin A \cos A$

$$\sin x° = 0 \qquad \text{or} \qquad 1 - 2\cos x° = 0$$

$$x = 0, 180, 360 \qquad\qquad \cos x° = \tfrac{1}{2}$$

$$x = 60 \text{ or } 360 - 60$$

$$= 60 \text{ or } 300$$

So $x = 0, 60, 180, 300, 360$.

$$a = \cos^{-1}\left(\tfrac{1}{2}\right)$$

$$= 60$$

> Exact value...

8

See *Polynomials and Quadratics* §3

a) <u>Method 1</u> Compensating...

$$2x^2 + 4x - 3 = 2(x^2 + 2x) - 3$$
$$= 2(x+1)^2 - 2 - 3 = 2(x+1)^2 - 5$$

This gives the correct x^2 and x terms, and an extra 2

Take off this extra 2.

<u>Method 2</u> Comparing coefficients...

$$2x^2 + 4x - 3 = a(x+b)^2 + c$$
$$= ax^2 + 2abx + ab^2 + c.$$

So $a = 2$, $2ab = 4$ and $ab^2 + c = -3$

$$b = \frac{4}{2a}$$ $$c = -3 - ab^2$$
$$= 1$$ $$= -5.$$

So $2x^2 + 4x - 3 = 2(x+1)^2 - 5$.

b) The turning point is $(-1, -5)$.

Remember:
The parabola $y = (x-p)^2 + q$ has turning point (p, q).

9

(a) See **Vectors** §11
(b) and (c) See **Polynomials and Quadratics** §9
(d) See **Vectors** §12

a)

$$\underline{u} \cdot \underline{v} = k^3 \times 1 + 1 \times 3k^2 - 1(k+2)$$
$$= k^3 + 3k^2 - k - 2.$$

So $k^3 + 3k^2 - k - 2 = 1$

$$k^3 + 3k^2 - k - 3 = 0.$$

b) Evaluate the expression for $k = -3$...

$$
\begin{array}{r|rrrr}
-3 & 1 & 3 & -1 & -3 \\
   &   & -3 & 0 & 3 \\
\hline
   & 1 & 0 & -1 & \boxed{0}
\end{array}
$$

or $(-3)^3 + 3 \times (-3)^2 - (-3) - 3$
$= -27 + 27 + 3 - 3$
$= 0.$

Since the value is zero, $(k+3)$ is a factor.

So $k^3 + 3k^2 - k - 3 = (k+3)(k^2-1)$
$= (k+3)(k+1)(k-1)$

> Either from the bottom row of the table or by inspection

c) We have $k^3 + 3k^2 - k - 3 = 0$

$$(k+3)(k+1)(k-1) = 0$$

$$k = -3, -1 \text{ or } 1.$$

From the question, $k > 0$ so $k = 1$.

d) $|\underline{u}| = \sqrt{1^2 + 1^2 + 3^2} = \sqrt{11}$, $|\underline{v}| = \sqrt{1^2 + 3^2 + (-1)^2} = \sqrt{11}$.

$\underline{u} \cdot \underline{v} = 1$ from part (a).

So $\cos\vartheta = \dfrac{\underline{u} \cdot \underline{v}}{|\underline{u}||\underline{v}|} = \dfrac{1}{11}$.

> Using:
> $\underline{a} \cdot \underline{b} = |\underline{a}||\underline{b}|\cos\vartheta$

10 *See **Exponentials and Logarithms** §6*

<u>Method 1</u> $y = a^x$

$$\log_4 y = \log_4 a^x$$

We know that $\log_4 y = 3$ when $x = 6$ from the diagram, so

$3 = \log_4 a^6$

$a^6 = 4^3$

$a = 4^{3/6}$

$\quad = 4^{1/2}$

$\quad = 2.$

Remember:
$x = \log_b y \Leftrightarrow y = b^x.$

<u>Method 2</u> The straight line has gradient $\frac{3}{6} = \frac{1}{2}$ and passes through the origin, so the equation is:

$$\log_4 y = \frac{1}{2}x$$

Just like $y = mx + c$ but with different axis labels.

$y = 4^{\frac{x}{2}}$

$\quad = \left(4^{1/2}\right)^x$

$\quad = 2^x.$

Remember:
$x = \log_a y \Leftrightarrow a^x = y$

So $a = 2.$ (comparing to $y = a^x$).

2006 Paper 2

1

See **Straight Lines** §3, §5 and §6

a $m_{PS} = \dfrac{6-0}{4-2} = \dfrac{6}{2} = 3$. So $m_{QS} = -\dfrac{1}{3}$ since PS and QS are perp.

The equation is $\quad y - 6 = -\dfrac{1}{3}(x-4)$

$$3y - 18 = -x + 4$$
$$x + 3y = 22.$$

b Q lies on QS and the x-axis. i.e. $y = 0$. So

$$x + 3 \times 0 = 22$$
$$x = 22. \quad Q \text{ is the point } (22,0).$$

Since PQRS is a parallelogram, $\overrightarrow{PS} = \overrightarrow{QR} = \begin{pmatrix} 2 \\ 6 \end{pmatrix}$.

So R is the point $(24, 6)$.

2

See **Polynomials and Quadratics** §2

For equal roots, $b^2 - 4ac = 0$ where $a = k$, $b = k$ and $c = 6$.

$$k^2 - 4 \times k \times 6 = 0$$
$$k^2 - 24k = 0$$
$$k(k - 24) = 0$$
$$\cancel{k = 0} \quad \text{or} \quad k = 24.$$

Question says $k \neq 0$.

So $k = 24$.

3

(a) See **Differentiation** §5
(b) See **Polynomials and Quadratics** §7

a $\frac{dy}{dx} = 2x - 14.$

At $x = 8$, $m_{tangent} = 2 \times 8 - 14 = 2.$

> Remember:
> $\frac{dy}{dx} = m_{tangent}.$

So the equation is $y - 5 = 2(x - 8)$

$$y - 5 = 2x - 16$$

$$2x - y - 11 = 0. \quad (\text{or } y = 2x - 11)$$

b At points of intersection of the line and parabola:

$$2x - 11 = -x^2 + 10x - 27$$

$$x^2 - 8x + 16 = 0.$$

$$(x - 4)^2 = 0$$

$$x - 4 = 0$$

$$x = 4.$$

> You could also use the discriminant to show there is just one solution.

Since there is only one solution, the line is a tangent to the parabola.

> Using the equation from part (a).

When $x = 4$, $y = 2 \times 4 - 11 = -3$. So Q is $(4, -3)$.

4

See **Circles** §1 and §3

$(x - 3)^2 + (y - 4)^2 = 25$: centre is $(3, 4)$, radius is 5 units.

$x^2 + y^2 - kx - 8y - 2k = 0$: centre is $\left(\frac{k}{2}, 4\right)$

So $\frac{k}{2} = 3$ i.e. $k = 6.$

The radius is $\sqrt{\left(-\frac{k}{2}\right)^2 + (-4)^2 - (-2k)} = \sqrt{9 + 16 + 12} = \sqrt{37}$

Since $\sqrt{37} > 5$, the radius of the larger circle is $\sqrt{37}$ units.

5 See *Integration* §3

$$y = \int \frac{dy}{dx}\, dx$$
$$= \int (4x - 6x^2)\, dx$$
$$= 2x^2 - 2x^3 + c.$$

When $x = -1$, $y = 9$ so $\quad 9 = 2 \times (-1)^2 - 2 \times (-1)^3 + c$
$$9 = 2 + 2 + c$$
$$c = 5.$$

So $\quad y = 2x^2 - 2x^3 + 5.$

6 See *Vectors* §7 and §3

a $\quad \vec{PQ} = q - p = \begin{pmatrix} 3 \\ 2 \\ -4 \end{pmatrix} - \begin{pmatrix} -1 \\ 2 \\ -1 \end{pmatrix} = \begin{pmatrix} 4 \\ 0 \\ -3 \end{pmatrix}.$

b $\quad |\vec{PQ}| = \sqrt{4^2 + (-3)^2} = \sqrt{25} = 5.$

c $\quad \frac{1}{5}\begin{pmatrix} 4 \\ 0 \\ -3 \end{pmatrix} = \begin{pmatrix} 4/5 \\ 0 \\ -3/5 \end{pmatrix}$ is a unit vector parallel to $\vec{PQ}$.

Remember: a unit vector has magnitude 1.

7 See *Functions and Graphs* §10

a $\quad y = f(x-4)$ is $y = f(x)$ shifted 4 to the right.

b $\quad y = 2 + f(x-4)$ is $y = f(x-4)$ shifted up 2

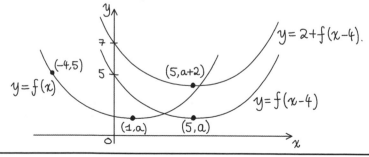

8

See **Trigonometry** $3 and $4

a **i** Using Pythagoras's Theorem:

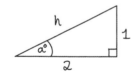

$$h = \sqrt{2^2 + 1^2} = \sqrt{5}.$$

$$\sin a° = \frac{opp.}{hyp.} = \frac{1}{\sqrt{5}}.$$

ii $\sin 2a° = 2\sin a° \cos a°$

$$= 2 \times \frac{1}{\sqrt{5}} \times \frac{2}{\sqrt{5}}$$

$$= \frac{4}{5}$$

b $\sin 3a° = \sin(2a° + a°)$

$$= \sin 2a° \cos a° + \cos 2a° \sin a°$$

$$= \frac{4}{5} \times \frac{2}{\sqrt{5}} + \frac{3}{5} \times \frac{1}{\sqrt{5}}$$

$$= \frac{11}{5\sqrt{5}} \quad \left(or \quad \frac{11\sqrt{5}}{25} \right)$$

Using Pythagoras's Theorem.

9

See **Further Calculus** $4

$$y = x^{-3} - \cos 2x$$

$$\frac{dy}{dx} = -3x^{-4} + 2\sin 2x$$

$$= -\frac{3}{x^4} + 2\sin 2x$$

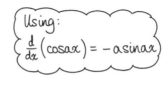

Using:
$$\frac{d}{dx}(\cos ax) = -a\sin ax$$

10

(a) See **Wave Functions** §2
(b) See **Further Calculus** §4 and **Trigonometry** §1

a

$7\sin x - 24\cos x = k\sin(x - a)$
$= k\sin x \cos a - k\cos x \sin a$
$= (k\cos a)\sin x - (k\sin a)\cos x$

Comparing coefficients: $k\sin a = 24$
$k\cos a = 7$

✓ S	A ✓		
T	C ✓		

So $k = \sqrt{7^2 + 24^2}$ and $\tan a = \dfrac{k\sin a}{k\cos a} = \dfrac{24}{7}$
$= \sqrt{625}$
$= 25.$ $\qquad a = \tan^{-1}\left(\dfrac{24}{7}\right) = 1\cdot287$ rads (to 3 d.p.)

So $7\sin x - 24\cos x = 25\sin(x - 1\cdot287).$

b

$\dfrac{dy}{dx} = 25\cos(x - 1\cdot287) = 1$

$\cos(x - 1\cdot287) = \dfrac{1}{25}$

Remember: $\dfrac{dy}{dx} = m_{tangent}.$

$x - 1\cdot287 = \cos^{-1}\left(\dfrac{1}{25}\right)$

*Remember:
Your calculator should
be in radian mode.*

$x - 1\cdot287 = 1\cdot531$

$x = 2\cdot818$ (to 3 d.p.)

11

See **Exponentials and Logarithms** §5

For 88% to be left, $A(t) = 0\cdot88A_0$. So:

$0\cdot88A_0 = A_0 e^{-0\cdot000124t}$

$e^{-0\cdot000124t} = 0\cdot88$

$\log_e e^{-0\cdot000124t} = \log_e 0\cdot88$

$-0\cdot000124t = \log_e 0\cdot88$

$t = \dfrac{\log_e 0\cdot88}{-0\cdot000124}$

$= 1030\cdot914$ (to 3 d.p.)

$> 1000.$

So the claim is true.

12

(a) See **Straight Lines** §1
(b) See **Differentiation** §10

a **i** $PS = 6 - x$ and $RS = 12 - \dfrac{8}{x}$.

ii $A = PS \times RS$

$= (6-x)\left(12 - \dfrac{8}{x}\right)$

$= 72 - \dfrac{48}{x} - 12x + 8$

$= 80 - 12x - \dfrac{48}{x}$.

b We have $1 \leqslant x \leqslant 4$. Extrema can occur at turning points or the endpoints of this closed interval.

Stationary points exist where $\dfrac{dA}{dx} = 0$.

$A = 80 - 12x - 48x^{-1}$

$\dfrac{dA}{dx} = -12 + 48x^{-2} = 0$

$\dfrac{48}{x^2} = 12$

$x^2 = 4$

$x = \pm 2$

$x = 2$ since $x > 0$.

When $x = 1$, $A = 80 - 12 \times 1 - 48 = 20$.

When $x = 2$, $A = 80 - 12 \times 2 - \dfrac{48}{2} = 32$.

When $x = 4$, $A = 80 - 12 \times 4 - \dfrac{48}{4} = 20$.

So the minimum value of A is 20 when $x = 1, 4$ and the maximum value is 32 when $x = 2$.

2007 Paper 1

1

See **Straight Lines** §3 and §6

<u>Method 1</u> $3x - y + 2 = 0$

$y = 3x + 2$

So $m = 3$.

Remember:
To extract the gradient, rearrange to the form $y = mx + c$.

Any line parallel to this has gradient 3.

The equation is $y - 4 = 3(x - (-1))$ using point $(-1, 4)$

$y - 4 = 3x + 3$

$3x - y + 7 = 0$.

<u>Method 2</u> The equation of the line has the form

$3x - y + c = 0$ and passes through $(-1, 4)$.

So $3(-1) - 4 + c = 0$

$-7 + c = 0$

$c = 7$.

So the line has equation $3x - y + 7 = 0$.

2

See **Vectors** §10

$\overrightarrow{BC} = 2\overrightarrow{AB}$

$\underline{c} - \underline{b} = 2(\underline{b} - \underline{a})$

$\underline{c} = 2\underline{b} - 2\underline{a} + \underline{b}$

$= 3\underline{b} - 2\underline{a}$

$= 3\begin{pmatrix} 1 \\ 3 \\ 2 \end{pmatrix} - 2\begin{pmatrix} -2 \\ 1 \\ -1 \end{pmatrix}$

$= \begin{pmatrix} 3 \\ 9 \\ 6 \end{pmatrix} - \begin{pmatrix} -4 \\ 2 \\ -2 \end{pmatrix}$

$= \begin{pmatrix} 7 \\ 7 \\ 8 \end{pmatrix}$.   So C is the point $(7, 7, 8)$.

Remember:
$\overrightarrow{AB} = \underline{b} - \underline{a}$

21

3.

See Functions and Graphs §3

a $g(f(x)) = g(x^2+1) = 1-2(x^2+1) = 1-2x^2-2 = -1-2x^2.$

b $g(g(x)) = g(1-2x) = 1-2(1-2x) = 1-2+4x = 4x-1.$

4

See Polynomials and Quadratics §2

For no real roots, $b^2-4ac < 0$ where $a=k, b=-1, c=-1$

$$(-1)^2 - 4k(-1) < 0$$
$$1 + 4k < 0$$
$$4k < -1$$
$$k < -\frac{1}{4}.$$

5.

See Circles §3 and §1

Large circle centred at B: $x^2 + y^2 - 14x - 16y + 77 = 0$

$$2g = -14 \qquad 2f = -16 \qquad c = 77.$$
$$g = -7 \qquad f = -8$$

Centre: $(-g, -f) = (7, 8).$

Radius: $\sqrt{g^2+f^2-c} = \sqrt{49+64-77} = \sqrt{36} = 6$ units.

So each small circle has radius $\frac{6}{3} = 2$ units.

Let D have coordinates $(x, 8)$. Then since each small circle has radius 2, $x = 7 + 4 \times 2 = 15$. So D is $(15, 8)$.

The x-coord. of B.   4 small radii.

The circle centred at D has equation

$$(x-15)^2 + (y-8)^2 = 4.$$

6

See **Trigonometry** §5

$$\sin 2x° = 6\cos x°$$
$$2\sin x°\cos x° = 6\cos x°$$
$$2\sin x°\cos x° - 6\cos x° = 0$$
$$2\cos x°(\sin x° - 3) = 0$$
$$\cos x°(\sin x° - 3) = 0$$

Using:
$$\sin 2A = 2\sin A\cos A.$$

$$\cos x° = 0 \qquad \text{or} \qquad \sin x° - 3 = 0$$
$$x = 90, 270. \qquad\qquad\qquad \sin x° = 3$$

No solutions
since $-1 \leq \sin x° \leq 1$.

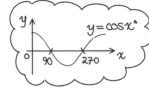

$y = \cos x°$

So $x = 90, 270$.

7

See **Sequences** – (a) §1 and §2, (b) §4

a
$$u_1 = \tfrac{1}{4}u_0 + 16 = \tfrac{1}{4} \times 0 + 16 = 16.$$
$$u_2 = \tfrac{1}{4}u_1 + 16 = \tfrac{1}{4} \times 16 + 16 = 4 + 16 = 20.$$
$$u_3 = \tfrac{1}{4} \times u_2 + 16 = \tfrac{1}{4} \times 20 + 16 = 5 + 16 = 21.$$

b *i* The sequence has a limit because $-1 < \tfrac{1}{4} < 1$.

ii **Method 1** $\quad k = \dfrac{b}{1-a}$ where $a = \tfrac{1}{4}$ and $b = 16$.

$$k = \frac{16}{1 - 1/4} = \frac{16}{3/4} = \frac{4}{3} \times 16 = \frac{64}{3}.$$

Method 2 As $n \to \infty$, $u_{n+1} = u_n = k$. So

$$k = \tfrac{1}{4}k + 16$$
$$\tfrac{3}{4}k = 16$$
$$k = \tfrac{4}{3} \times 16$$
$$= \frac{64}{3}$$

2007

8

(a) and (b) See **Polynomials and Quadratics** §9
(c) See **Integration** §5

a Evaluate y when $x = 3$...

$$3 \ \big|\ 1 \quad -4 \quad 1 \quad 6$$
$$\ 3 \quad -3 \quad -6$$
$$\ \overline{1 \quad -1 \quad -2 \ \big|\ 0}$$

OR

$$y = 3^3 - 4 \times 3^2 + 3 + 6$$
$$= 27 - 36 + 9$$
$$= 0.$$

So the curve crosses the x-axis at $(3,0)$.

b Since $x = 3$ is a root, $(x - 3)$ is a factor.

So $x^3 - 4x^2 + x + 6 = (x - 3)(x^2 - x - 2)$
$$= (x - 3)(x + 1)(x - 2).$$

> Either from the bottom row of the table or by inspection.

So A has coordinates $(2, 0)$.

The shaded area is

$$\int_0^2 (x^3 - 4x^2 + x + 6)\,dx = \left[\frac{x^4}{4} - \frac{4x^3}{3} + \frac{x^2}{2} + 6x \right]_0^2$$

$$= \frac{2^4}{4} - \frac{4 \times 2^3}{3} + \frac{2^2}{2} + 6 \times 2$$

$$= 4 - \frac{32}{3} + 2 + 12$$

$$= 18 - 10\tfrac{2}{3}$$

$$= 7\tfrac{1}{3} \text{ square units}$$

$$\left(\text{or } \frac{22}{3} \text{ square units.} \right)$$

9

See **Differentiation** §7, §8 and §9

a) When $x = 0$, $f(0) = 3 \times 0 - 0^3 = 0$.

When $y = 0$, $3x - x^3 = 0$

$$x(3 - x^2) = 0$$

$$x = 0 \qquad \text{or} \qquad 3 - x^2 = 0$$

$$x = \pm\sqrt{3}.$$

So the curve passes through $(-\sqrt{3}, 0)$, $(0, 0)$ and $(\sqrt{3}, 0)$.

b) Stationary points exist where $f'(x) = 0$.

$$f'(x) = 3 - 3x^2 = 0$$

$$x^2 = 1$$

$$x = \pm 1.$$

When $x = 1$, $y = 3 \times 1 - 1^3 = 3 - 1 = 2$. $(1, 2)$

When $x = -1$, $y = 3 \times (-1) - (-1)^3 = -3 + 1 = -2$. $(-1, -2)$.

Method 1 Nature table...

x	-1^-	-1	-1^+	1^-	1	1^+
$f'(x)$	$-$	0	$+$	$+$	0	$-$
Sketch	↘	—	↗	↗	—	↘

Method 2 The second derivative test... $f''(x) = -6x$.

$$f(-1) > 0, \quad f(1) < 0.$$

So $(-1, -2)$ is a minimum turning point and $(1, 2)$ is a maximum turning point.

c)

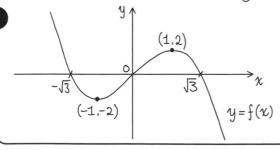

10

See **Further Calculus** §4

$$y = (3x^2+2)^{1/2}$$

$$\frac{dy}{dx} = \frac{1}{2}(3x^2+2)^{-1/2} \times \frac{d}{dx}(3x^2+2)$$

Remember the Chain Rule

$$= \frac{1}{2}(3x^2+2)^{-1/2} \times 6x$$

$$= \frac{3x}{\sqrt{3x^2+2}}.$$

11

See **Wave Functions** §6

a

$$\sqrt{3}\cos x + \sin x = k\cos(x-a)$$
$$= k\cos x \cos a + k\sin x \sin a$$
$$= (k\cos a)\cos x + (k\sin a)\sin x$$

Comparing coefficients:

$$k\sin a = 1$$
$$k\cos a = \sqrt{3}$$

$$\begin{array}{c|c} \checkmark\ S & A\ \checkmark\checkmark \\ \hline T & C\ \checkmark \end{array}$$

So $k = \sqrt{1^2 + \sqrt{3}^2}$ and $\tan a = \dfrac{k\sin a}{k\cos a} = \dfrac{1}{\sqrt{3}}$.

$$= \sqrt{4}$$
$$= 2$$

$$a = \frac{\pi}{6}.$$

Exact value...

2 $\quad \pi/6 \quad$ $\sqrt{3}$ $\quad \pi/3 \quad$ 1

So $\sqrt{3}\cos x + \sin x = 2\cos\left(x - \dfrac{\pi}{6}\right).$

b

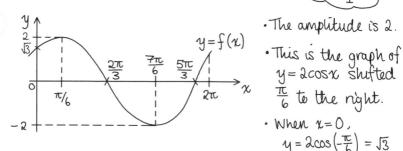

$y = f(x)$

- The amplitude is 2.
- This is the graph of $y = 2\cos x$ shifted $\frac{\pi}{6}$ to the right.
- When $x = 0$,
  $y = 2\cos\left(-\frac{\pi}{6}\right) = \sqrt{3}$

2007 Paper 2

1

See **Vectors** §7 and §12

a $G(0, 2, 2)$.

b From the diagram

$$\mathbf{p} = \tfrac{1}{2}\mathbf{g} = \tfrac{1}{2}\begin{pmatrix} 0 \\ 2 \\ 2 \end{pmatrix} = \begin{pmatrix} 0 \\ 1 \\ 1 \end{pmatrix}.$$

$$\mathbf{q} = \mathbf{b} + \tfrac{1}{2}\overrightarrow{BG} = \mathbf{b} + \tfrac{1}{2}(\mathbf{g} - \mathbf{b}) = \tfrac{1}{2}(\mathbf{b} + \mathbf{g}) = \tfrac{1}{2}\begin{pmatrix} 2 \\ 4 \\ 2 \end{pmatrix} = \begin{pmatrix} 1 \\ 2 \\ 1 \end{pmatrix}.$$

c $|\mathbf{p}| = \sqrt{1^2 + 1^2} = \sqrt{2}$, $\quad |\mathbf{q}| = \sqrt{1^2 + 2^2 + 1^2} = \sqrt{6}$.

$\mathbf{p} \cdot \mathbf{q} = 0 \times 1 + 1 \times 2 + 1 \times 1 = 3$

So $\quad \cos P\hat{O}Q = \dfrac{\mathbf{p} \cdot \mathbf{q}}{|\mathbf{p}||\mathbf{q}|}$

Using:
$$\mathbf{a} \cdot \mathbf{b} = |\mathbf{a}||\mathbf{b}|\cos\theta$$

$$= \dfrac{3}{\sqrt{2}\sqrt{6}}$$

Exact value…

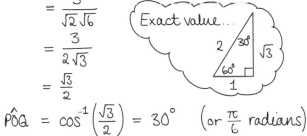

$$= \dfrac{3}{2\sqrt{3}}$$

$$= \dfrac{\sqrt{3}}{2}$$

$$P\hat{O}Q = \cos^{-1}\left(\dfrac{\sqrt{3}}{2}\right) = 30° \quad \left(\text{or } \dfrac{\pi}{6} \text{ radians}\right)$$

2

See **Trigonometry** – (a) §3, (b) §4

Using Pythagoras's Theorem…

$$\sin c = \dfrac{1}{\sqrt{5}} \quad \cos c = \dfrac{2}{\sqrt{5}}$$

$$\sin d = \dfrac{1}{\sqrt{10}} \quad \cos d = \dfrac{3}{\sqrt{10}}$$

cont…

a $\sin(c+d) = \sin c . \cos d + \cos c \sin d$

$$= \frac{1}{\sqrt{5}} \times \frac{3}{\sqrt{10}} + \frac{2}{\sqrt{5}} \times \frac{1}{\sqrt{10}}$$

$$= \frac{3+2}{\sqrt{5}\sqrt{10}}$$

$$= \frac{5}{5\sqrt{2}}$$

$$= \frac{1}{\sqrt{2}}$$

b i $\sin 2c = 2\sin c \cos c = 2 \times \frac{1}{\sqrt{5}} \times \frac{2}{\sqrt{5}} = \frac{4}{5}$.

ii $\cos 2d = 2\cos^2 d - 1$

$$= 2 \times \frac{9}{10} - 1$$

$$= \frac{9}{5} - \frac{5}{5}$$

$$= \frac{4}{5}.$$

> Any of the three formulae for $\cos 2d$ could be used here.

3

See **Circles** §4

To find points of intersection, put $y = 6 - 2x$ into the equation of the circle:

$$x^2 + (6-2x)^2 + 6x - 4(6-2x) - 7 = 0$$

$$x^2 + 36 - 24x + 4x^2 + 6x - 24 + 8x - 7 = 0$$

$$5x^2 - 10x + 5 = 0$$

$$x^2 - 2x + 1 = 0$$

$$(x-1)^2 = 0$$

$$x = 1$$

> You could also use the discriminant to show there is just one solution.

Since there is only one solution, the line is a tangent to the circle.

When $x = 1$, $y = 6 - 2 \times 1 = 4$.

So the point of contact is $(1,4)$.

4

(a) See **Functions and Graphs** §9 and §10
(b) See **Trigonometry** §1

a The amplitude is 2, so $a = 2$.

There are three complete waves in $360°$ so $b = 3$.

The graph is the same as $y = a\sin(bx°)$ but shifted down 1.

So $c = -1$.

b
$$2\sin(3x°) - 1 = 0$$
$$\sin(3x°) = \tfrac{1}{2}$$

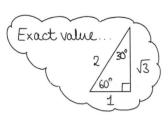

Exact value...

$$3x = 30 \quad \text{or} \quad 180 - 30$$
$$3x = 30 \quad \text{or} \quad 150$$
$$x = 10 \quad \text{or} \quad 50$$

From the diagram, the x-coordinate of P is 50.

5

(a) See **Differentiation** §5 or **Polynomials and Quadratics** §7
(b) See **Polynomials and Quadratics** §7
(c) See **Circles** §6

a <u>Method 1</u> $\dfrac{dy}{dx} = 2 \times \tfrac{1}{2}x - 8 = x - 8$.

Remember:
$$\dfrac{dy}{dx} = m_{tangent}.$$

$m_{tangent} = 4$ i.e. $\dfrac{dy}{dx} = 4$

So $x - 8 = 4$
$$x = 12.$$

When $x = 12$, $y = \tfrac{1}{2} \times 12^2 - 8 \times 12 + 34 = 72 - 96 + 34 = 10$

So Q is the point $(12, 10)$.

cont...

Method 2 The tangent has the form $y = 4x + c$. There is just one point of intersection with the parabola.

So $\frac{1}{2}x^2 - 8x + 34 = 4x + c$

$\frac{1}{2}x^2 - 12x + 34 - c = 0$ has discriminant zero.

So $x = -\dfrac{b}{2a}$ where $a = \frac{1}{2}$, $b = -12$

From the quadratic formula:
$$x = \dfrac{-b \pm \sqrt{b^2 - 4ac}}{2a}$$

$= \dfrac{12}{2 \times \frac{1}{2}} = 12.$

When $x = 12$, $y = \frac{1}{2} \times 12^2 - 8 \times 12 + 34 = 72 - 96 + 34 = 10$.

So Q is the point $(12, 10)$.

b P has the same y-coordinate as Q, so

$\frac{1}{2}x^2 - 8x + 34 = 10$ ← The y-coord. of P.

$\frac{1}{2}x^2 - 8x - 24 = 0$

$x^2 - 16x - 48 = 0$ multiplying through by 2.

$(x - 4)(x - 12) = 0$

$x = 4$ or $x = 12$.

So P is the point $(4, 10)$.

c C has x-coordinate 8 by symmetry.

Let C be the point $(8, y)$.

$m_{CQ} \times m_{tgt.} = -1$ since CQ is a radius.

So $m_{CQ} = -\dfrac{1}{4}$. However, $m_{CQ} = \dfrac{10 - y}{12 - 8} = \dfrac{10 - y}{4}$.

So $\dfrac{10 - y}{4} = -\dfrac{1}{4}$

$10 - y = -1$

$y = 11$.

So C is the point $(8, 11)$.

2007

6

See **Differentiation** §12 or **Polynomials and Quadratics** §3 and §1

a **i** Using Pythagoras's Theorem: $ST = \sqrt{10^2 + 10^2} = \sqrt{200} = 10\sqrt{2}$.

ii

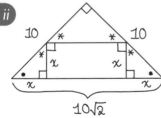

$10\sqrt{2}$

- • $= 45°$ since the large triangle is isosceles.

- ∗ $= 45°$ since the angles in a triangle and on a straight line sum to $180°$.

So the shaded area is $A = $ length × breadth
$$= (10\sqrt{2} - 2x)x$$
$$= 10\sqrt{2}\,x - 2x^2 \text{ square metres}$$

b **Method 1**   Stationary points exist where $\dfrac{dA}{dx} = 0$.

$$\frac{dA}{dx} = 10\sqrt{2} - 4x = 0$$
$$4x = 10\sqrt{2}$$
$$x = \frac{10\sqrt{2}}{4}$$
$$= \frac{5\sqrt{2}}{2}.$$

Nature...

x	$\frac{5\sqrt{2}}{2}^-$	$\frac{5\sqrt{2}}{2}$	$\frac{5\sqrt{2}}{2}^+$
$\frac{dA}{dx}$	+	0	−
Sketch	/	—	\

or $\dfrac{d^2A}{dx^2} = -4$.

Hence $x = \dfrac{5\sqrt{2}}{2}$ gives the maximum area.

cont...

2007

Method 2 Completing the square...

$$A = -2x^2 + 10\sqrt{2}\,x$$
$$= -2\left(x^2 - 5\sqrt{2}\,x\right)$$
$$= -2\left(x - \frac{5\sqrt{2}}{2}\right)^2 + 2\left(\frac{5\sqrt{2}}{2}\right)^2$$

The x-coordinate of the turning point is $x = \frac{5\sqrt{2}}{2}$.

The turning point is a maximum since the x^2-coefficient is negative.

Hence $x = \frac{5\sqrt{2}}{2}$ gives the maximum area.

When the breadth is $\frac{5\sqrt{2}}{2}$ metres, the length is

$$10\sqrt{2} - 2 \times \frac{5\sqrt{2}}{2} = 5\sqrt{2} \text{ metres.}$$

7

See **Further Calculus** §6

$$\int_0^2 \sin(4x+1)\,dx$$

$$= \left[-\tfrac{1}{4}\cos(4x+1)\right]_0^2$$

Using
$$\int \sin ax\,dx = -\tfrac{1}{a}\cos ax + c.$$

$$= -\tfrac{1}{4}\cos(4\times2+1) + \tfrac{1}{4}\cos(4\times0+1)$$

$$= -\tfrac{1}{4}\cos9 + \tfrac{1}{4}\cos1$$

$$= 0.363 \quad (\text{to 3 d.p.})$$

Remember:
We must work in radians when doing calculus.

2007

32

8

See **Exponentials and Logarithms** §5

Put $x = a$ and $y = 0$ into the equation:

$$0 = \log_3 (a-1) - 2 \cdot 2$$
$$\log_3 (a-1) = 2 \cdot 2$$
$$a - 1 = 3^{2 \cdot 2}$$
$$a = 3^{2 \cdot 2} + 1$$
$$= 12 \cdot 212 \quad (\text{to 3 d.p.})$$

Remember:
$$x = \log_a y \Leftrightarrow a^x = y$$

9

See **Exponentials and Logarithms** §7

a $y = a^{-x}$. Reflect in the y-axis.

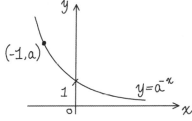

b $y = a^{1-x} = a \times a^{-x}$. The graph is as above but scaled by a in the y-direction — each y-coordinate is multiplied by $a > 0$.

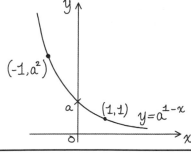

Also, when $x = 1$,
$$y = a^{1-1} = a^0 = 1.$$
So the curve passes through the point $(1,1)$.

10

(a) See **Polynomials and Quadratics** §5

(b) See **Integration** §3

a **i** The curve $y = f'(x)$ has roots $x = 2$ and $x = 4$. So $x - 2$ and $x - 4$ are factors of $f'(x)$.

So $a = 2$ and $b = 4$ (or vice versa).

ii We know that $f'(0) = 6$, so

$$k(0-4)(0-2) = 6$$
$$8k = 6$$
$$k = \frac{6}{8}$$
$$= \frac{3}{4}.$$

b
$$f(x) = \int f'(x)\, dx$$
$$= \frac{3}{4} \int (x-2)(x-4)\, dx$$
$$= \frac{3}{4} \int (x^2 - 6x + 8)\, dx$$
$$= \frac{3}{4}\left(\frac{x^3}{3} - 3x^2 + 8x\right) + c$$

From the question, $f(0) = 6$. So $c = 6$. Therefore:

$$f(x) = \frac{3}{4}\left(\frac{x^3}{3} - 3x^2 + 8x\right) + 6 = \frac{1}{4}x^3 - \frac{9}{4}x^2 + 6x + 6.$$

11

See **Exponentials and Logarithms** – (a) and (b) §5, (c) §6

a Put $x = a$ and $y = 6$ in the equation:

$$6 = 3 \times 4^a$$
$$4^a = 2$$
$$a = \frac{1}{2} \text{ since } 4^{1/2} = \sqrt{4} = 2.$$

cont...

b Put $x = -\frac{1}{2}$ and $y = b$ in the equation:

$b = 3 \times 4^{-\frac{1}{2}}$

$= \frac{3}{\sqrt{4}}$

$= \frac{3}{2}$.

> Remember:
> $u^{-m} = \frac{1}{u^m}$.

c <u>Method 1</u> $y = 3 \times 4^x$

$\log_{10} y = \log_{10}(3 \times 4^x)$ taking $\log_{10}$ on both sides

$= \log_{10} 3 + \log_{10} 4^x$

$= \log_{10} 3 + x \log_{10} 4$

> Remember:
> • $\log_a xy = \log_a x + \log_a y$.
> • $k\log_a x = \log_a x^k$

So $\log_{10} y = (\log_{10} 4)x + \log_{10} 3$

The gradient is $\log_{10} 4$. (Comparing to $y = mx + c$.)

<u>Method 2</u> Start with $\log_{10} y = Px + Q$ and find P and Q.

$\log_{10} y = Px + Q$

$y = 10^{Px+Q}$

$y = 10^Q \times 10^{Px}$

Comparing to $y = 3 \times 4^x$...

$10^Q = 3$ and $10^{Px} = 4^x$

$Q = \log_{10} 3$ $(10^P)^x = 4^x$

$10^P = 4$

$P = \log_{10} 4$.

The gradient is $P = \log_{10} 4$.

1

*See **Differentiation** §2*

$$y = \frac{x^3 - x}{x^2} = \frac{x^3}{x^2} - \frac{x}{x^2} = x - x^{-1}.$$

$$\frac{dy}{dx} = 1 + x^{-2} = 1 + \frac{1}{x^2}.$$

Remember:
$$\frac{x^a}{x^b} = x^{a-b}.$$

B

2

*See **Functions and Graphs** §3*

$$g(f(x)) = g(2x-3) = (2x-3)^2 = 4x^2 - 12x + 9.$$

A

3

*See **Integration** §1 and §2*

$$\int \frac{1}{3\sqrt{x}} dx = \int x^{-1/3} dx$$

$$= \frac{x^{2/3}}{2/3} + C$$

$$= \frac{3}{2} x^{2/3} + C$$

Remember:
$$\frac{a}{b/c} = a \times \frac{c}{b}$$

C

4

*See **Vectors** §3*

$$d_{AB}^2 = (2 - (-1))^2 + (3 - (-4))^2 + (-2 - 0)^2$$

$$= 3^2 + 7^2 + (-2)^2$$

$$= 9 + 49 + 4$$

$$= 62.$$

So $d_{AB} = \sqrt{62}$.

C

5

See *Sequences* §1 and §2

$u_0 = -1$

$u_1 = 3u_0 - 4 = 3 \times (-1) - 4 = -3 - 4 = -7.$

$u_2 = 3u_1 - 4 = 3 \times (-7) - 4 = -21 - 4 = -25.$

A

6

See *Functions and Graphs* §10

$y = -3 - f(x) = -f(x) - 3.$

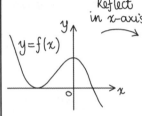
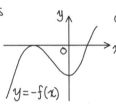
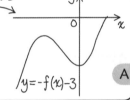

A

7

See *Polynomials and Quadratics* §3 and §1

The turning point is $(4, -5)$.
Since the x^2 coefficient is $3 > 0$,
the parabola is concave up, i.e.
$\cup$ - shaped.
So the turning point is a minimum.

Remember:
The parabola $y = a(x-p)^2 + q$
has turning point (p, q).

C

8

See *Trigonometry* §4

$\sin 2x° = 2 \sin x° \cos x°$
$= 2 \times \dfrac{2\sqrt{2}}{3} \times \dfrac{1}{3}$
$= \dfrac{4\sqrt{2}}{9}$

$\sin x° = \dfrac{\text{opposite}}{\text{hypotenuse}} = \dfrac{2\sqrt{2}}{3}.$

$\cos x° = \dfrac{\text{adjacent}}{\text{hypotenuse}} = \dfrac{1}{3}.$

A

9

See **Trigonometry** §3

$\sin(a-b) = \sin a \cos b - \cos a \sin b$

$\qquad = \dfrac{1}{\sqrt{5}} \times \dfrac{4}{\sqrt{17}} - \dfrac{2}{\sqrt{5}} \times \dfrac{1}{\sqrt{17}}$

$\qquad = \dfrac{4-2}{\sqrt{5}\sqrt{17}}$

$\qquad = \dfrac{2}{\sqrt{85}}$

Remember: $\sqrt{x}\sqrt{y} = \sqrt{xy}$

$\sin a = \dfrac{\text{opp.}}{\text{hyp.}} = \dfrac{1}{\sqrt{5}}$

$\cos a = \dfrac{\text{adj.}}{\text{hyp.}} = \dfrac{2}{\sqrt{5}}$

$\sin b = \dfrac{1}{\sqrt{17}}$, $\cos b = \dfrac{4}{\sqrt{17}}$

B

10

See **Circles** §3

The radius is $\sqrt{g^2 + f^2 - c}$ where $g = 4$, $f = -3$ and $c = -12$.

i.e. $\sqrt{4^2 + (-3)^2 - (-12)} = \sqrt{16 + 9 + 12} = \sqrt{37}$.

C

11

See **Vectors** §9

Since points P, Q and R are collinear, $\overrightarrow{QR} = k\overrightarrow{PQ}$ for some constant k.

$\overrightarrow{PQ} = q - p = \begin{pmatrix} 5 \\ 13 \\ 13 \end{pmatrix} - \begin{pmatrix} 1 \\ 3 \\ 7 \end{pmatrix} = \begin{pmatrix} 4 \\ 10 \\ 6 \end{pmatrix}$

$\overrightarrow{QR} = r - q = \begin{pmatrix} s \\ 33 \\ 25 \end{pmatrix} - \begin{pmatrix} 5 \\ 13 \\ 13 \end{pmatrix} = \begin{pmatrix} s-5 \\ 20 \\ 12 \end{pmatrix}$

So each component of $\overrightarrow{QR}$ is twice the component of $\overrightarrow{PQ}$

So $\quad s - 5 = 2 \times 4$

$\qquad s = 8 + 5$

$\qquad s = 13$.

C

12

See **Polynomials and Quadratics** §3

Method 1

$$2x^2 - 12x + 11 = 2(x^2 - 6x) + 11$$
$$= 2(x-3)^2 - 18 + 11$$
$$= 2(x-3)^2 - 7. \text{ So } c = -7.$$

Method 2 Comparing coefficients...

$$2x^2 - 12x + 11 = 2(x-b)^2 + c$$
$$= 2(x^2 - 2bx + b^2) + c$$
$$= 2x^2 - 4bx + 2b^2 + c.$$

So $4b = 12$ and $2b^2 + c = 11$

$$b = 3.$$
$$c = 11 - 2 \times 3^2$$
$$c = 11 - 18$$
$$c = -7.$$

B

13

See **Integration** §3

$$y = \int \frac{dy}{dx}\, dx$$
$$= \int (3x^2 + 9x + 1)\, dx$$
$$= \frac{3x^3}{3} + \frac{9x^2}{2} + x + c$$
$$= x^3 + \frac{9}{2}x^2 + x + c.$$

The curve passes through the origin, so $y = 0$ when $x = 0$.

Hence $c = 0$ and so $y = x^3 + \frac{9}{2}x^2 + x$.

A

SQP 1

14 *See **Polynomials and Quadratics** §2*

For equal roots, $b^2 - 4ac = 0$ where $a = 1$, $b = -3$ and $c = k$.

$$(-3)^2 - 4 \times 1 \times k = 0$$
$$9 - 4k = 0$$
$$k = \frac{9}{4}.$$

D

15 *See **Circles** §6*

The centre of the circle is $(3, 4)$.

So $m_{radius} = \dfrac{4-2}{3-(-1)} = \dfrac{2}{4} = \dfrac{1}{2}$

$\therefore m_{tgt} = -2$ since the radius and tangent are perpendicular.

A

16 *See **Further Calculus** §6*

$$\int_0^{\pi/6} (4\cos 2x)\, dx = \left[4 \times \frac{1}{2} \sin 2x \right]_0^{\pi/6}$$

Using:
$\int \cos ax\, dx = \frac{1}{a}\sin ax + c.$

$$= \left[2\sin 2x \right]_0^{\pi/6}$$
$$= 2\sin\frac{\pi}{3} - 2\sin 0$$

Exact value…

$$= 2 \times \frac{\sqrt{3}}{2} - 0$$
$$= \sqrt{3}.$$

C

17 *See **Functions and Graphs** §9 and §10*

There are 2 complete waves in 2π radians, so $p = 2$.
The graph is $y = \sin(2x)$ shifted up 1, so $q = 1$.

A

18 See **Vectors** §11 and §13

The angle ϑ between $\underline{a}$ and $\underline{c}$ is such that $\cos\vartheta = \dfrac{adj}{hyp} = \dfrac{3}{5}$.

So $\underline{a}.\underline{c} = |\underline{a}||\underline{c}|\cos\vartheta = 3 \times 5 \times \dfrac{3}{5} = 9$. So (1) is true.

Since $\underline{a}$ and $\underline{b}$ are perpendicular, $\underline{a}.\underline{b} = 0$. So (2) is false. **B**

19 See **Exponentials and Logarithms** §5

Method 1

$$\log_3 t - \log_3 5 = 2$$
$$\log_3\left(\frac{t}{5}\right) = 2$$
$$\frac{t}{5} = 3^2$$
$$t = 5 \times 9$$
$$= 45$$

Remember:
- $\log_a x - \log_a y = \log_a \dfrac{x}{y}$.
- $y = \log_a x \Leftrightarrow x = a^y$.

Method 2

$$\log_3 t = 2 + \log_3 5$$
$$= 2\log_3 3 + \log_3 5$$
$$= \log_3 3^2 + \log_3 5$$
$$= \log_3(9 \times 5)$$
$$= \log_3 45$$
$$t = 45.$$

Remember:
- $\log_a a = 1$
- $\log_a x + \log_a y = \log_a xy$
- $\log_a x = \log_a y \Leftrightarrow x = y$

D

20 See **Exponentials and Logarithms** §5

$$3^k = e^4$$
$$\log_e 3^k = \log_e e^4 \qquad \text{taking } \log_e \text{ on both sides}$$
$$k \times \log_e 3 = 4$$
$$k = \frac{4}{\log_e 3}.$$

Remember:
- $\log_a x^k = k\log_a x$
- $\log_a a = 1$

C

21

See **Sequences** §2 and §4

a Product A : $\quad u_{n+1} = 0 \cdot 3 u_n + 300 \qquad u_0 = k,$ a constant

⤷ 70% of the germs are removed, so 30% remain.

Product B: $\quad v_{n+1} = 0 \cdot 2 v_n + 350 \qquad v_0 = k.$

b As $n \to \infty$, u_n and v_n both tend to limits because $-1 < 0 \cdot 3 < 1$ and $-1 < 0 \cdot 2 < 1.$

<u>Method 1</u> $\quad l_A = \dfrac{300}{1 - 0 \cdot 3} = \dfrac{300}{0 \cdot 7} = \dfrac{3000}{7}.$

$\qquad\qquad l_B = \dfrac{350}{1 - 0 \cdot 2} = \dfrac{350}{0 \cdot 8} = \dfrac{3500}{8}.$

<u>Method 2</u> As $n \to \infty$, $u_{n+1} = u_n = l_A$ and $v_{n+1} = v_n = l_B.$

$\qquad l_A = 0 \cdot 3 l_A + 300 \qquad\qquad l_B = 0 \cdot 2 l_B + 350$

$\qquad 0 \cdot 7 l_A = 300 \qquad\qquad\qquad 0 \cdot 8 l_B = 350$

$\qquad\qquad l_A = \dfrac{300}{0 \cdot 7} \qquad\qquad\qquad l_B = \dfrac{350}{0 \cdot 8}$

$\qquad\qquad\quad = \dfrac{3000}{7} \qquad\qquad\qquad\quad = \dfrac{3500}{8}$

To compare, put over a common denominator:

$\quad l_A = \dfrac{3000}{7} = \dfrac{3000 \times 8}{56} = \dfrac{24\,000}{56}$

$\quad l_B = \dfrac{3500}{8} = \dfrac{3500 \times 7}{56} = \dfrac{24\,500}{56}$

So $l_A < l_B.$

<u>or</u> carry out division:

A : $\quad 7 \overline{\smash{)}3000 \cdot 0000} \quad$ so the number of germs present will settle around 428.

$\qquad\qquad 428 \cdot 571$

B : $\quad 8 \overline{\smash{)}3500 \cdot 00} \quad$ so the number of germs present will settle around 437.

$\qquad\qquad 437 \cdot 5$

So product A is more effective in the long term.

SQP 1

22

See **Differentiation** §7, §8 and §9

a Stationary points exist where $\frac{dy}{dx} = 0$.

$$\frac{dy}{dx} = 3x^2 - 18x + 24 = 0$$

$$x^2 - 6x + 8 = 0 \quad (\div 3)$$

$$(x-2)(x-4) = 0.$$

$$x - 2 = 0 \quad \text{or} \quad x - 4 = 0$$

$$x = 2 \qquad\qquad x = 4.$$

When $x = 2$, $y = 2^3 - 9 \times 2^2 + 24 \times 2 - 20$

$$= 8 - 36 + 48 - 20$$

$$= 0. \quad (2, 0)$$

Or use synthetic division.

When $x = 4$, $y = 4^3 - 9 \times 4^2 + 24 \times 4 - 20$

$$= 64 - 9 \times 16 + 96 - 20$$

$$= 140 - 144$$

$$= -4 \quad (4, -4).$$

Method 1 Nature table:

x	2^-	2	2^+	4^-	4	4^+
$(x-2)$	$-$	0	$+$	$+$		$+$
$(x-4)$	$-$		$-$	$-$	0	$+$
$\frac{dy}{dx}$	$+$	0	$-$	$-$	0	$+$
Sketch	$/$	$-$	$\backslash$	$\backslash$	$-$	$/$

Method 2 Second derivative test: $\frac{d^2y}{dx^2} = 6x - 18$.

When $x = 2$, $\frac{d^2y}{dx^2} = -6 < 0$. When $x = 4$, $\frac{d^2y}{dx^2} = 6 > 0$.

So $(2, 0)$ is a maximum turning point.
$(4, -4)$ is a minimum turning point.

cont...

SQP 1

b **i** $(x-2)^2(x-5) = (x^2-4x+4)(x-5)$
$$= x^3-4x^2+4x-5x^2+20x-20$$
$$= x^3-9x^2+24x-20.$$

ii To find the x-axis intercepts, put $y=0$:

$$x^3-9x^2+24x-20 = 0$$
$$(x-2)^2(x-5) = 0$$

$$x-2=0 \quad \text{or} \quad x-5=0$$
$$x=2 \qquad\qquad x=5.$$

So the curve passes through $(2,0)$ and $(5,0)$.

To find the y-axis intercept, put $x=0$: $y=-20$.
So the curve passes through $(0,-20)$.

Using this information and the stationary points:

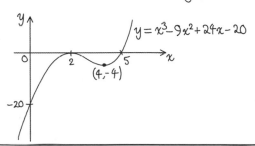

23

See **Polynomials and Quadratics** §11 and §9

Equate to find points of intersection...
$$x^3+5x^2-36x+32 = -x^2+x+2$$
$$x^3+6x^2-37x+30 = 0.$$

cont...

Method 1 By inspection: $(x-1)(x^2+7x-30) = 0$

$$(x-1)(x+10)(x-3) = 0$$

$$x = 1 \text{ or } x = -10 \text{ or } x = 3.$$

Method 2 Evaluate the expression for $x = 1$:

$$
\begin{array}{c|cccc}
1 & 1 & 6 & -37 & 30 \\
  &   & 1 & 7   & -30 \\
\hline
  & 1 & 7 & -30 & 0
\end{array}
$$

Since the remainder is 0, $x = 1$ is a root so $(x-1)$ is a factor.

$$x^3 + 6x^2 - 37x + 30 = 0$$
$$(x-1)(x^2 + 7x - 30) = 0$$

The coefficients of the other factor come from the bottom row of the table.

$$(x-1)(x+10)(x-3) = 0.$$

$$x = 1 \text{ or } x = -10 \text{ or } x = 3.$$

From the diagram, A has $x = -10$, B has $x = 1$ and C has $x = 3$

---

24   See **Trigonometry** §5

$$\sin^2 p - \sin p + 1 = 1 - \sin^2 p$$
$$2\sin^2 p - \sin p = 0$$
$$\sin p (2\sin p - 1) = 0$$

Remember:
$$\sin^2 x + \cos^2 x = 1$$
so $\cos^2 x = 1 - \sin^2 x$

$\sin p = 0$ or $2\sin p - 1 = 0$

$p = 0, \pi, 2\pi$

We want $\frac{\pi}{2} < p < \pi$

$\sin p = \frac{1}{2}$

$p = \pi - \frac{\pi}{6}$

$= \frac{5\pi}{6}$

We want $\frac{\pi}{2} < p < \pi$.

Exact value...

So $p = \frac{5\pi}{6}$.

SQP 1 Paper 2

1

See **Straight Lines** (a) §7, (b) §8, (c) §10, (d) §3

a) $N = \text{midpoint}_{AB} = \left(\dfrac{2+10}{2}, \dfrac{1+1}{2}\right) = (6,1).$

$m_{CN} = \dfrac{1-7}{6-4} = \dfrac{-6}{2} = -3.$

So the equation is $\quad y - 1 = -3(x-6) \quad$ using $N(6,1)$

$$y - 1 = -3x + 18$$
$$3x + y - 19 = 0.$$

b) $m_{BC} = \dfrac{7-1}{4-10} = \dfrac{6}{-6} = -1.$ So $m_{AD} = 1$ since $AD \perp BC.$

$$\text{(i.e. } m_{BC} \times m_{AD} = -1)$$

So the equation is $\quad y - 1 = 1(x - 2) \quad$ using $A(2,1).$

$$x - y - 1 = 0.$$

Solve simultaneously...

Method 1 Eliminating y:

$$3x + y - 19 = 0 \quad\text{————①}$$
$$x - y - 1 = 0 \quad\text{————②}$$

①+②: $4x - 20 = 0$

$$x = 5$$

Method 2 Rearrange both equations for y and equate:

$$19 - 3x = x - 1$$
$$4x = 20$$
$$x = 5$$

When $x = 5$, $y = 5 - 1 = 4$. So P has coordinates $(5,4)$.

d) $m_{PQ} = \dfrac{1-4}{8-5} = \dfrac{-3}{3} = -1 = m_{BC}$ from part (b).

So PQ and BC are parallel.

SQP 1

2

See **Vectors** §7, §3 and §12

a The lengths of the edges are as follows...

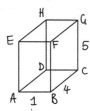

- A and B only differ in the first coordinate, so the length of AB is the difference in the first coordinate.
- Similar for BC = AD.
- C has coordinates $(2,7,9)$ so GC = AE = 5.

Note: It's not necessary to show any of this working.

So AB = 1, AD = 4, AE = 5.

b $\vec{HB} = \underline{b} - \underline{h} = \begin{pmatrix} 2 \\ 3 \\ 4 \end{pmatrix} - \begin{pmatrix} 1 \\ 7 \\ 9 \end{pmatrix} = \begin{pmatrix} 1 \\ -4 \\ -5 \end{pmatrix}$.

$\vec{HC} = \underline{c} - \underline{h} = \begin{pmatrix} 2 \\ 7 \\ 4 \end{pmatrix} - \begin{pmatrix} 1 \\ 7 \\ 9 \end{pmatrix} = \begin{pmatrix} 1 \\ 0 \\ -5 \end{pmatrix}$.

Remember: $\vec{AB} = \underline{b} - \underline{a}$

You could just write these down from the diagram.

$|\vec{HB}| = \sqrt{1^2 + (-4)^2 + (-5)^2} = \sqrt{42}$.
$|\vec{HC}| = \sqrt{1^2 + (-5)^2} = \sqrt{26}$.

Method 1 $\cos B\hat{H}C = \dfrac{\vec{HB} \cdot \vec{HC}}{|\vec{HB}||\vec{HC}|}$

Using: $\underline{a} \cdot \underline{b} = |\underline{a}||\underline{b}|\cos\theta$

$= \dfrac{1 \times 1 - 4 \times 0 - 5 \times (-5)}{\sqrt{42}\sqrt{26}}$

$B\hat{H}C = \cos^{-1}\left(\dfrac{26}{\sqrt{42}\sqrt{26}}\right)$

$= 38.11°$ (to 2 d.p.)

OR 0.665 rads (to 3 d.p.)

cont...

48

Method 2 We have:

So $\cos B\hat{H}C = \dfrac{42+26-16}{2\sqrt{42}\sqrt{26}}$

$= \dfrac{26}{\sqrt{42}\sqrt{26}}$

(Remember the cosine rule:
$\cos A = \dfrac{b^2+c^2-a^2}{2bc}$)

So $B\hat{H}C = 38.\underline{11}°$ (to 2 d.p.) OR 0.665 rads (to 3 d.p.)

3

See **Wave Functions** §2 and §5

SQP 1

a) $5\sin x° - 12\cos x° = k\sin(x°-a°)$

$= k\sin x° \cos a° - k\cos x° \sin a°.$

$= (k\cos a°)\sin x° - (k\sin a°)\cos x°.$

Comparing coefficients: $\begin{array}{l} k\sin a° = 12 \\ k\cos a° = 5 \end{array}$

$\begin{array}{c|c} \checkmark S & A \checkmark \\ \hline T & C \checkmark \end{array}$

So $k = \sqrt{12^2+5^2}$ and $\tan a° = \dfrac{k\sin a°}{k\cos a°} = \dfrac{12}{5}$

$= \sqrt{169}$

$= 13$

$a = \tan^{-1}\left(\dfrac{12}{5}\right) = 67.38$ (to 2 d.p.)

So $5\sin x° - 12\cos x° = 13\sin(x° - 67.38°).$

b) $5\sin x° - 12\cos x° = 6.5$

$13\sin(x° - 67.38°) = 6.5$

$\sin(x° - 67.38°) = 0.5$ $\quad\begin{array}{c|c} \checkmark S & A \checkmark \\ \hline T & C \end{array}$ $\quad \sin^{-1}(0.5) = 30°$

$x - 67.38 = 30$ or $180 - 30$

$x = 97.38$ or 217.38 (to 2 d.p.)

4

(a) See **Differentiation** §5
(b) See **Circles** §5
(c) See **Vectors** §10

a $\frac{dy}{dx} = 4x - 2$. (Remember: $\frac{dy}{dx} = m_{tangent}$)

When $x = 1$, $m_{tangent} = 4 \times 1 - 2 = 2$.

Using $P(1,3)$, the equation is $y - 3 = 2(x - 1)$
$$y - 3 = 2x - 2$$
$$2x - y + 1 = 0.$$

b Put $y = 2x + 1$ into the equation of the circle...

$$x^2 + (2x+1)^2 + 8(2x+1) + 11 = 0$$
$$x^2 + 4x^2 + 4x + 1 + 16x + 8 + 11 = 0$$
$$5x^2 + 20x + 20 = 0$$
$$x^2 + 4x + 4 = 0$$
$$(x+2)^2 = 0$$
$$x = -2.$$

(You could have used the discriminant to show that there is only one solution)

Since there is only one solution, there is only one point of intersection. Hence the line is a tangent to the circle.

When $x = -2$, $y = 2 \times (-2) + 1 = -4 + 1 = -3$.
So the point of contact is $Q(-2, -3)$.

cont...

SQP 1

c QP has equation $y = 2x + 1$.
So when $x = 0$, $y = 1$.

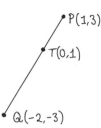

P(1,3)

T(0,1)

Method 1

$\overrightarrow{TP} = \begin{pmatrix} 1 \\ 2 \end{pmatrix}$, $\overrightarrow{QT} = \begin{pmatrix} 2 \\ 4 \end{pmatrix} = 2\overrightarrow{TP}$ Q(-2,-3)

So T divides $\overrightarrow{QP}$ in the ratio $2:1$.

Method 2

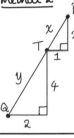

By Pythagoras's Theorem:

$x^2 = 2^2 + 1^2$, so $x = \sqrt{5}$.

$y^2 = 4^2 + 2^2$, so $y = \sqrt{20} = 2\sqrt{5}$.

So T divides $\overrightarrow{QP}$ in the ratio $2:1$.

SQP 1

5

(a) See **Integration** §6
(b) See **Differentiation** §12 or **Polynomials and Quadratics** §3

a Points of intersection...

$$x^2 = 6x + 16$$

$$x^2 - 6x - 16 = 0$$

$$(x + 2)(x - 8) = 0$$

$$x + 2 = 0 \text{ or } x - 8 = 0.$$

$$x = -2 \qquad x = 8$$

cont...

The shaded area is given by

$$\int_{-2}^{8} (\text{upper} - \text{lower})\, dx$$

$$= \int_{-2}^{8} (6x + 16 - x^2)\, dx$$

$$= \left[3x^2 + 16x - \frac{x^3}{3} \right]_{-2}^{8}$$

$$= \left(3 \times 8^2 + 16 \times 8 - \frac{8^3}{3} \right) - \left(3 \times (-2)^2 + 16 \times (-2) - \frac{(-2)^3}{3} \right)$$

$$= \frac{448}{3} + \frac{52}{3}$$

$$= \frac{500}{3} \quad \left(= 166\tfrac{2}{3} \right).$$

So the area is $\frac{500}{3}$ square units.

b We want to maximise $A(x) = -5x^2 + 30x + 80$.

Method 1   Stationary points exist where $A'(x) = 0$.

$$A'(x) = -10x + 30 = 0$$
$$x = \frac{30}{10}$$
$$= 3$$

Then $A(3) = -5 \times 3^2 + 30 \times 3 + 80 = 125$.

Nature:

x	3^-	3	3^+
$A'(x)$	+	0	−
Sketch	/	−	\

So the maximum area is 125 square units.

cont...

SQP 1

Method 2 Completing the square ...

$$A(x) = -5(x^2 - 6x) + 80$$
$$= -5(x-3)^2 + 45 + 80$$
$$= -5(x-3)^2 + 125.$$

The turning point is $(3, 125)$ and is a maximum since $-5 < 0$ so the parabola is concave down $(\cap)$.

So the maximum area is 125 square units.

As a proportion of the total area it is $\dfrac{125}{500/3} = \dfrac{375}{500} = \dfrac{3}{4}$.

6

See **Exponentials and Logarithms** §5

SQP 1

a $A(1600) = \frac{1}{2} A_0$ After 1600 years, the amount has halved.

$$A_0 e^{-1600k} = \frac{1}{2} A_0$$

$$e^{-1600k} = \frac{1}{2}$$

$$-1600k = \log_e\left(\frac{1}{2}\right)   \text{Taking } \log_e \text{ on both sides}$$

$$k = -\frac{\log_e\left(\frac{1}{2}\right)}{1600}$$

$$= 0 \cdot 0004332 \text{ (to 4 s.f.)}$$

b **Method 1** $A(3200) = A_0 \times e^{(-0 \cdot 0004332 \times 3200)}$ (Remember the brackets on your calculator.)

$$= 0 \cdot 250 A_0 \text{ (to 3 d.p.)}$$

So after 3200 years, we are left with 25%.

Method 2 Let $A_0 = 100$ since we start with 100%.

Then $A(3200) = 100 e^{(-0 \cdot 0004332 \times 3200)}$

$$= 25 \cdot 001 \text{ (to 3 d.p.)}$$

$$= 25 \text{ (to the nearest whole number)}$$

So after 3200 years, we are left with 25%.

7

See **Trigonometry** §4

From the diagram, $\cos 2x° = \dfrac{adj.}{hyp.} = \dfrac{6}{10} = \dfrac{3}{5}$.

$$\cos 2x° = 2\cos^2 x° - 1 = \frac{3}{5}$$

$$2\cos^2 x° = \frac{8}{5}$$

$$\cos^2 x° = \frac{8}{10}$$

$$\cos^2 x = \frac{4}{5}$$

$$\cos x° = \pm \frac{2}{\sqrt{5}}.$$

Since x is acute, $\cos x° > 0$ so $\cos x° = \dfrac{2}{\sqrt{5}}$.

From the diagram, $\cos x° = \dfrac{6}{BD}$

$$BD = \frac{6}{2/\sqrt{5}}$$

$$= 3\sqrt{5} \quad \text{units}.$$

SQP 1

SQP 2 Paper 1

1

See **Straight Lines** §3

$$m_{PQ} = \frac{p-(-5)}{7-4} = \frac{p+5}{3}.$$

So $\frac{p+5}{3} = 3$

$p+5 = 9$

$p = 4.$

B

2

See **Sequences** §2

$u_1 = u_0 + 5 = -3 + 5 = 2$

$u_2 = u_1 + 5 = 2 + 5 = 7$

C

3

See **Straight Lines** §6 and §5

$3y = -2x + 1$

$y = -\frac{2}{3}x + \frac{1}{3}.$

> Remember:
> To extract the gradient,
> rearrange to the form
> $y = mx + c.$

So the gradient is $m = -\frac{2}{3}.$

Any line perpendicular has gradient $m_\perp = \frac{3}{2}$, since $m \times m_\perp = -1.$

C

4

See **Polynomials and Quadratics** §9

The remainder is

$f(-3) = (-3)^3 - (-3)^2 - 5 \times (-3) - 3$

$= -27 - 9 + 15 - 3$

$= -24.$

> You could have used
> synthetic division

A

SQP 2

55

5

See **Polynomials and Quadratics** §3

Method 1 Compensating...

$$x^2 - 16x + 27 = (x-8)^2 - 64 + 27 = (x-8)^2 - 37. \text{ So } q = -37.$$

This gives the correct x^2 and x terms, and an extra 64

Take off this extra 64

Method 2 Comparing coefficients...

$$x^2 - 16x + 27 = (x+p)^2 + q$$
$$= x^2 + 2px + p^2 + q.$$

So $\quad 2p = -16 \quad$ and $\quad p^2 + q = 27$
$$p = -8 \qquad\qquad q = 27 - p^2$$
$$= -37.$$

A

6

See **Further Calculus** §4

Using the chain rule,

$$\frac{d}{dx}(8 - 2x^2)^{2/3} = \frac{2}{3}(8 - 2x^2)^{-1/3} \times \frac{d}{dx}(8 - 2x^2)$$

$$= \frac{2}{3}(8 - 2x^2)^{-1/3} \cdot (-4x)$$

$$= -\frac{8}{3}(8 - 2x^2)^{-1/3}.$$

A

7

See **Polynomials and Quadratics** §9

Since the remainder is zero, $(x-1)$ is a factor, i.e.

$$f(x) = (x-1)(x^2 - 4x - 5)$$
$$= (x-1)(x+1)(x-5).$$

D

8

See **Sequences** §4

__Method 1__ $\quad l = \dfrac{b}{1-a}\quad$ with $\ a = 0.4$ and $b = 3$

$l = \dfrac{3}{1-0.4} = \dfrac{3}{0.6} = \dfrac{30}{6} = 5.$

__Method 2__ As $n \to \infty$, $u_{n+1} = u_n = l$.

So $l = 0.4l + 3$

$\quad 0.6l = 3$

$\qquad l = \dfrac{3}{0.6} = \dfrac{30}{6} = 5.$

C

9

See **Trigonometry** §1

$\tan x = -\sqrt{3}$

$\begin{array}{c|c} \pi-a & a \\ \hline \text{S} & \text{A} \\ \text{T} & \text{C} \\ \hline \pi+a & 2\pi-a \end{array}$

$a = \tan^{-1}(\sqrt{3})$

$\quad = \dfrac{\pi}{3}$

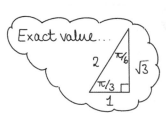

Exact value...

So $x = \pi - \dfrac{\pi}{3}$ or $2\pi - \dfrac{\pi}{3}$.

$\quad = \dfrac{2\pi}{3}\qquad$ or $\quad\dfrac{5\pi}{3}$.

C

SQP 2

10

See **Vectors** §10

$\overrightarrow{PQ} = \underline{q} - \underline{p} = \begin{pmatrix} -1 \\ 8 \\ 3 \end{pmatrix} - \begin{pmatrix} -3 \\ 4 \\ 7 \end{pmatrix} = \begin{pmatrix} 2 \\ 4 \\ -4 \end{pmatrix}$

$\overrightarrow{QR} = \underline{r} - \underline{q} = \begin{pmatrix} 0 \\ 10 \\ 1 \end{pmatrix} - \begin{pmatrix} -1 \\ 8 \\ 3 \end{pmatrix} = \begin{pmatrix} 1 \\ 2 \\ -2 \end{pmatrix}$

So $\overrightarrow{PQ} = 2\overrightarrow{QR}$, i.e. $\dfrac{PQ}{QR} = \dfrac{2}{1}$. Hence Q divides PR in the ratio 2:1.

A

1

See **Straight Lines** §6 and §3

$2y = x$

$y = \frac{1}{2}x$. So $m = \frac{1}{2}$.

Since $m = \tan p°$,

$\tan p° = \frac{1}{2}$

$p = \tan^{-1}\left(\frac{1}{2}\right)$

Remember:
To extract the gradient, rearrange to the form
$y = mx + c$.

A

2

See **Differentiation** §6

$g'(x) = x^2 + 2x + 1$

$= (x+1)^2$

$\geqslant 0$.

Since $g'(x) \geqslant 0$ for all x, g is never decreasing.

D

3

See **Exponentials and Logarithms** §3

$\log_2(x+1) - 2\log_2 3 = \log_2(x+1) - \log_2 3^2$

$= \log_2(x+1) - \log_2 9$

$= \log_2\left(\frac{x+1}{9}\right)$

Remember:
• $k\log_a x = \log_a x^k$.
• $\log_a x - \log_a y = \log_a \frac{x}{y}$.

A

4

See **Functions and Graphs** §10

$y = -g(x)$ is $y = g(x)$ reflected in the x-axis.

$3 - g(x) = -g(x) + 3$.
So $y = 3 - g(x)$ is
$y = -g(x)$ shifted up
by 3.

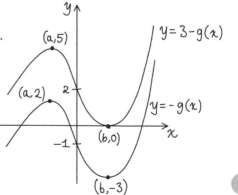

D

15

See **Vectors** §7 and §10

__Method 1__ $\underline{t} = \underline{p} + \frac{1}{2}\overrightarrow{PQ}$

$$= \underline{p} + \frac{1}{2}(\underline{q} - \underline{p})$$

$$= \frac{1}{2}(\underline{p} + \underline{q})$$

$$= \frac{1}{2}\left(\begin{pmatrix} 1 \\ 3 \\ -1 \end{pmatrix} + \begin{pmatrix} 2 \\ 5 \\ 1 \end{pmatrix}\right)$$

$$= \begin{pmatrix} 3/2 \\ 4 \\ 0 \end{pmatrix}.$$

__Method 2__ Using the midpoint formula, T is

$$\left(\frac{1+2}{2}, \frac{3+5}{2}, \frac{-1+1}{2}\right) = \left(\frac{3}{2}, 4, 0\right).$$

So $\underline{t} = \begin{pmatrix} 3/2 \\ 4 \\ 0 \end{pmatrix}.$

B

16

See **Vectors** §7

$$\overrightarrow{AD} = 4\overrightarrow{AB}$$

$$\underline{d} - \underline{a} = 4(\underline{b} - \underline{a})$$

$$\underline{d} = 4\underline{b} - 4\underline{a} + \underline{a}$$

$$= 4\underline{b} - 3\underline{a}$$

$$= 4\begin{pmatrix} -1 \\ 8 \\ 3 \end{pmatrix} - 3\begin{pmatrix} -3 \\ 4 \\ 7 \end{pmatrix}$$

$$= \begin{pmatrix} -4 \\ 32 \\ 12 \end{pmatrix} - \begin{pmatrix} -9 \\ 12 \\ 21 \end{pmatrix}$$

$$= \begin{pmatrix} 5 \\ 20 \\ -9 \end{pmatrix}.$$ So D has coordinates $(5, 20, -9)$.

D

SQP 2

17

See **Polynomials and Quadratics** §5

Since $(3, -18)$ lies on the parabola,

$-18 = k \times 3 \times (3 - 6)$

$-18 = -9k$

$k = 2$.

C

18

See **Further Calculus** §4

$\frac{dy}{dx} = 3 \times (-5) \sin 5x$

$= -15 \sin 5x$.

Using: $\frac{d}{dx}(\cos ax) = -a \sin ax$.

B

19

See **Further Calculus** §5

$\int (4x+1)^{1/2} dx = \frac{(4x+1)^{3/2}}{4 \times \frac{3}{2}} + c$

$= \frac{1}{6}(4x+1)^{3/2} + c$.

Remember:

$\int (ax+b)^n dx = \frac{(ax+b)^{n+1}}{a(n+1)} + c$

A

20

See **Integration** §4

$\int_0^1 (3x+1)^{-1/2} dx = \left[\frac{2}{3}\sqrt{3x+1} \right]_0^1$

$= \frac{2}{3} \times 2 - \frac{2}{3} \times 1$

$= \frac{2}{3}$.

A

21

See **Differentiation** – (a) §7 and §8, (b) §9

a Stationary points exist where $\frac{dy}{dx} = 0$.

$$\frac{dy}{dx} = 3x^2 + 6x - 9 = 0$$
$$x^2 + 2x - 3 = 0$$
$$(x+3)(x-1) = 0$$
$$x = -3 \quad \text{or} \quad x = 1$$

When $x = -3$, $\quad y = (-3)^3 + 3 \times (-3)^2 - 9 \times (-3) + 5$
$$= -27 + 27 + 27 + 5$$
$$= 32. \qquad (-3, 32)$$

When $x = 1$, $\quad y = 1 + 3 - 9 + 5 = 0 \qquad (1, 0)$

Method 1 Nature table:

x	-3^-	-3	-3^+	1^-	1	1^+
$(x+3)$	$-$	0	$+$	$+$		$+$
$(x-1)$	$-$		$-$	$-$	0	$+$
$\frac{dy}{dx}$	$+$	0	$-$	$-$	0	$+$
Sketch	$/$	$-$	$\backslash$	$\backslash$	$\_$	$/$

Method 2 Second derivative test: $\quad \frac{d^2y}{dx^2} = 6x + 6$.

$$f''(-3) = -12 < 0 \quad \text{and} \quad f''(1) = 12 > 0$$

So $(-3, 32)$ is a maximum turning point
$\quad (1, 0)$ is a minimum turning point.

b When $x = 0$, $y = 5$. So $(0, 5)$ lies on the curve.
Using the given information, and the stationary points,

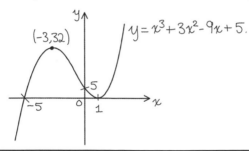

$$y = x^3 + 3x^2 - 9x + 5.$$

22

See **Exponentials and Logarithms** §5

$$\log_x 8 + \log_x 4 = 5$$
$$\log_x 32 = 5$$
$$x^5 = 32$$
$$x = \sqrt[5]{32}$$
$$= 2.$$

Remember:
- $\log_a u + \log_a v = \log_a uv$
- $\log_a u = v \iff a^v = u.$

23

See **Trigonometry** §4 and §5

$$\sin 2x - \cos x = 0$$
$$2\sin x \cos x - \cos x = 0$$
$$\cos x (2\sin x - 1) = 0$$

Using: $\sin 2A = 2\sin A \cos A$

$$\cos x = 0 \quad \text{or} \quad 2\sin x - 1 = 0$$
$$\sin x = \frac{1}{2}$$

$$\begin{array}{c|c} \frac{\pi - a}{S} & \frac{a}{A} \\ \hline T & C \\ \pi + a & 2\pi - a \end{array}$$

$$a = \sin^{-1}\left(\frac{1}{2}\right)$$
$$= \frac{\pi}{6}$$

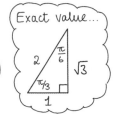

Exact value...

$$x = \frac{\pi}{2} \quad \text{or} \quad \frac{3\pi}{2} \quad \text{or} \quad \frac{\pi}{6} \quad \text{or} \quad \frac{5\pi}{6}.$$

24

See **Trigonometry** §3 and §4

From the diagram: $\hat{DEA} = 2x + 90.$

So $\cos(\hat{DEA}°) = \cos(2x° + 90°)$

Remember: $\cos(u° + 90°)$
$= -\sin u°.$

Note: you could have used the addition formula.

$$= -\sin(2x°)$$
$$= -2\sin x° \cos x°$$
$$= -2 \times \frac{1}{\sqrt{10}} \times \frac{3}{\sqrt{10}}$$
$$= -\frac{6}{10} = -\frac{3}{5}.$$

By Pythagoras's Theorem:
$$l^2 = 3^2 + 1^2$$
$$l = \sqrt{10}.$$

SQP 2

25

See **Integration** §3

$$f(x) = \int f'(x)\, dx$$
$$= \int 6x(x-2)\, dx$$
$$= \int (6x^2 - 12x)\, dx$$
$$= \frac{6x^3}{3} - \frac{12x^2}{2} + c$$
$$= 2x^3 - 6x^2 + c.$$

We know $f(1) = 4$, i.e. $2 \times 1^3 - 6 \times 1^2 + c = 4$
$$-4 + c = 4$$
$$c = 8.$$

So $f(x) = 2x^3 - 6x^2 + 8$.

1

See **Vectors** §12

$$|\overrightarrow{QP}| = \sqrt{(-1)^2 + 3^2 + (-2)^2} = \sqrt{1+9+4} = \sqrt{14}$$

$$|\overrightarrow{QR}| = \sqrt{(-5)^2 + 1^2 + 1^2} = \sqrt{25+1+1} = \sqrt{27}$$

$$\overrightarrow{QP}.\overrightarrow{QR} = -1 \times (-5) + 3 \times 1 - 2 \times 1 = 5 + 3 - 2 = 6.$$

$$\cos P\hat{Q}R = \frac{\overrightarrow{QP}.\overrightarrow{QR}}{|\overrightarrow{QP}||\overrightarrow{QR}|}$$

$$= \frac{6}{\sqrt{14}\sqrt{27}}$$

Using:
$$\underline{a}.\underline{b} = |\underline{a}||\underline{b}|\cos\theta$$

$$P\hat{Q}R = \cos^{-1}\left(\frac{6}{\sqrt{14}\sqrt{27}}\right)$$

$$= 72.02° \quad (\text{to } 2 \text{ d.p.})$$

$$\text{or } 1.257 \text{ rads} \quad (\text{to } 3 \text{ d.p.})$$

SQP 2

2

See **Polynomials and Quadratics** §2

Given $2x^2 + px - 3 = 0$, let $a = 2$, $b = p$ and $c = -3$.

$$b^2 - 4ac = p^2 - 4 \times 2 \times (-3)$$

$$= p^2 + 24.$$

But $p^2 \geqslant 0$ for all p, so $p^2 + 24 > 0$ for all p.

Hence the equation has real (and distinct) roots for all p.

3

See **Differentiation** §5

a

$$y = 6x^2 - x^3$$
$$\frac{dy}{dx} = 12x - 3x^2$$

Remember:
$$\frac{dy}{dx} = m_{tangent}.$$

Since the tangent at P has gradient 12:

$$12x - 3x^2 = 12$$
$$3x^2 - 12x + 12 = 0$$
$$x^2 - 4x + 4 = 0$$
$$(x-2)^2 = 0$$
$$x = 2.$$

b When $x = 2$, $y = 6 \times 2^2 - 2^3 = 24 - 8 = 16$. So P is $(2, 16)$.

The equation of the tangent is
$$y - 16 = 12(x-2)$$
$$y - 16 = 12x - 24$$
$$12x - y - 8 = 0.$$

4

See **Wave Functions** §5

a
$$3\cos x° + 5\sin x° = k\cos(x° - a°)$$
$$= k\cos x° \cos a° + k\sin x° \sin a°.$$
$$= (k\cos a°)\cos x° + (k\sin a°)\sin x°.$$

Comparing coefficients:
$$k\sin a° = 5$$
$$k\cos a° = 3$$

So $k = \sqrt{5^2 + 3^2}$
$$= \sqrt{25 + 9}$$
$$= \sqrt{34}$$

and $\tan a° = \dfrac{k\sin a°}{k\cos a°} = \dfrac{5}{3}$

$$a = \tan^{-1}\left(\frac{5}{3}\right) = 59.04 \text{ (to 2 d.p.)}$$

So $3\cos x° + 5\sin x° = \sqrt{34}\cos(x° - 59.04°)$.

cont...

SQP 2

b $\quad 3\cos x° + 5\sin x° = 4 \qquad\qquad 0 \leqslant x \leqslant 90$

$\sqrt{34}\cos(x° - 59.04°) = 4 \qquad -59.04 \leqslant x - 59.04 \leqslant 30.96^{*}$

$\cos(x° - 59.04°) = \dfrac{4}{\sqrt{34}}$

$a = \cos^{-1}\left(\dfrac{4}{\sqrt{34}}\right)$

$= 46.69 \ (2\,\text{d.p.})$

$x - 59.04 = 46.69 \quad\text{or}\quad 360 - 46.69$

$\qquad\qquad = \cancel{46.69} \quad\text{or}\quad \cancel{313.31}$

$\qquad\qquad\qquad\qquad\qquad\text{too large (see}^{*})$

Look 360° backwards:

$x - 59.04 = 46.69 - 360 \quad\text{or}\quad 313.31 - 360$

$\qquad\qquad = -\cancel{313.31} \quad\text{or}\quad -46.69$

$\qquad\qquad\quad\text{too small}$

So $\quad x = -46.69 + 59.04$

$\qquad\quad = 12.35.$

5

See **Differentiation** §11

a

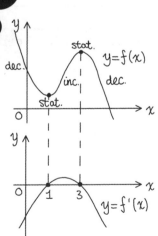

dec: $f(x)$ is decreasing
so $f'(x) < 0$, i.e.
$f'(x)$ is below the x-axis.

inc: $f(x)$ is increasing
so $f'(x) > 0$, i.e.
$f'(x)$ is above the x-axis.

stat: $f(x)$ is stationary
so $f'(x) = 0$, i.e.
$f'(x)$ lies on the x-axis.

SQP 2

6

(a) See **Circles** §6 or §5
(b) See **Circles** §5
(c) See **Straight Lines** §1

a Method 1

The centre is $A(6,1)$.

$$m_{AP} = \frac{-1-1}{5-6} = \frac{-2}{-1} = 2.$$

> Using:
> $x^2 + y^2 + 2gx + 2fy + c = 0$
> has centre $(-g, -f)$.

So $m_{PT} = -\frac{1}{2}$ since the radius and tangent are perpendicular.

The equation of PT is:

$$y + 1 = -\frac{1}{2}(x - 5) \qquad \text{using point } P(5, -1).$$
$$2y + 2 = -(x - 5) \qquad \text{multiplying by 2.}$$
$$2y + 2 = -x + 5$$
$$x + 2y = 3.$$

Method 2 Write $x + 2y = 3$ as $x = 3 - 2y$ and substitute into the equation of the circle:

$$(3 - 2y)^2 + y^2 - 12(3 - 2y) - 2y + 32 = 0$$
$$9 - 12y + 4y^2 + y^2 - 36 + 24y - 2y + 32 = 0$$
$$5y^2 + 10y + 5 = 0$$
$$y^2 + 2y + 1 = 0$$
$$(y + 1)^2 = 0.$$

Since there is only one solution, the line is a tangent. Check that P lies on the line: $x = 3 - 2 \times (-1) = 5$.

cont...

SQP 2

6 Line PT has equation $x = 3 - 2y$. To find points of intersection, substitute this into the equation of the circle:

$$(3 - 2y)^2 + y^2 + 10(3 - 2y) + 2y + 6 = 0$$
$$9 - 12y + 4y^2 + y^2 + 30 - 20y + 2y + 6 = 0$$
$$5y^2 - 30y + 45 = 0$$
$$y^2 - 6y + 9 = 0$$
$$(y - 3)^2 = 0$$
$$y = 3$$

You could also use the discriminant to show there is just one solution.

Since there is only one solution, the line is a tangent.

When $y = 3$, $x = 3 - 2 \times 3 = -3$. So Q is the point $(-3, 3)$.

$$\text{So } PQ = \sqrt{(-3 - 5)^2 + (3 - (-1))^2}$$
$$= \sqrt{64 + 16}$$
$$= \sqrt{80}$$
$$= 4\sqrt{5}$$

7

*See **Differentiation** §12*

a We are told that the surface area is 12 square units.

The surface area is given by:

$$2 \times \text{short side} + 2 \times \text{long side} + \text{base}$$
$$= 2 \times 2x \times h + 2 \times x \times h + 2x \times x$$
$$= 6xh + 2x^2 = 12$$

$$\text{So } 6xh = 12 - 2x^2$$
$$3xh = 6 - x^2$$
$$h = \frac{6 - x^2}{3x}.$$

The volume is $V(x) = 2x \times x \times h = 2x^2 \cdot \frac{6 - x^2}{3x} = \frac{2}{3}x(6 - x^2).$

cont...

b Stationary values exist where $V'(x) = 0$.

$$V(x) = \tfrac{2}{3}x(6 - x^2) = 4x - \tfrac{2}{3}x^3.$$

$$V'(x) = 4 - 2x^2 = 0$$

$$2x^2 = 4$$

$$x^2 = 2$$

$$x = \sqrt{2} \quad (\text{no "} \pm \text{" since lengths are positive})$$

Check this gives a maximum...

x	$\sqrt{2}^{-}$	$\sqrt{2}$	$\sqrt{2}^{+}$
$V'(x)$	+	0	−
Sketch	/	−	\

Hence the maximum volume occurs when $x = \sqrt{2}$.

8

See **Exponentials and Logarithms** §5

SQP 2

a We are told that $A_{1000} = 600$, i.e:

$$A_0 e^{-0.002 \times 1000} = 600$$

$$A_0 e^{-2} = 600$$

$$A_0 = \frac{600}{e^{-2}}$$

$$= 600 e^2$$

$$= 4433.43 \text{ micrograms (to 2 d.p.)} \quad \boxed{cont...}$$

b

$$A_t = \tfrac{1}{2} A_0$$

$$A_0 e^{-0.002t} = \tfrac{1}{2} A_0$$

$$e^{-0.002t} = \tfrac{1}{2}$$

$$\log_e e^{-0.002t} = \log_e \tfrac{1}{2} \qquad \text{(taking } \log_e \text{ on both sides)}$$

$$-0.002t = \log_e \tfrac{1}{2}$$

$$t = -\frac{\log_e \tfrac{1}{2}}{0.002}$$

Remember:
- $\log_a x^k = k\log_a x$
- $\log_a a = 1$.

$$= 346.57 \text{ years (to 2 d.p.)}$$

9

See *Integration* §6

To find the limits of integration...

$$2x - \tfrac{1}{2} x^2 = 1.5$$

$$4x - x^2 = 3 \qquad \text{multiplying through by 2.}$$

$$x^2 - 4x + 3 = 0$$

$$(x-1)(x-3) = 0$$

$$x = 1 \quad \text{or} \quad x = 3.$$

The shaded area is given by:

$$\int_1^3 (\text{upper} - \text{lower})\, dx = \int_1^3 \left(2x - \tfrac{1}{2} x^2 - 1.5\right) dx$$

$$= \left[x^2 - \tfrac{1}{6} x^3 - 1.5x\right]_1^3$$

$$= 9 - \tfrac{27}{6} - 4.5 - \left(1 - \tfrac{1}{6} - 1.5\right)$$

$$= \tfrac{2}{3} \text{ square units.}$$

1

See **Sequences** §2

$u_{11} = 0.3u_{10} + 6 = 0.3 \times 10 + 6 = 3 + 6 = 9.$
$u_{12} = 0.3u_{11} + 6 = 0.3 \times 9 + 6 = 2.7 + 6 = 8.7.$

C

2

See **Circles** §1

Since the x-axis is a tangent, the radius is 6 units.

Therefore the equation is
$$(x-(-7))^2 + (y-6)^2 = 6^2$$
$$(x+7)^2 + (y-6)^2 = 36.$$

The circle with centre (a,b) and radius r has equation:
$$(x-a)^2 + (y-b)^2 = r^2.$$

D

3

See **Vectors** §13

$\underline{u} \cdot \underline{v} = (k \times 0) + (-1 \times 4) + (1 \times k)$
$= k - 4.$

Since $\underline{u}$ and $\underline{v}$ are perpendicular, $\underline{u} \cdot \underline{v} = 0.$

So $k - 4 = 0$ i.e. $k = 4.$

C

4

See **Sequences** §4

Method 1 $l = \dfrac{b}{1-a}$ with $a = 0.4$ and $b = -240.$

$l = \dfrac{-240}{1-0.4} = -\dfrac{240}{0.6} = -\dfrac{2400}{6} = -400.$

Method 2   As $n \to \infty$, $u_{n+1} = u_n = l.$

So $l = 0.4l - 240$
$0.6l = -240$
$l = -\dfrac{240}{0.6} = -\dfrac{2400}{6} = -400.$

B

5
See **Circles** §6

$m_{radius} = \dfrac{9-5}{7-2} = \dfrac{4}{5}$.

So $m_{tangent} = -\dfrac{5}{4}$ since the radius and tangent are perpendicular.

The equation of the tangent is:

$y - 9 = -\dfrac{5}{4}(x-7)$ 　　　　using point $(7,9)$

A

6
See **Trigonometry** §1

$2\sin x - \sqrt{3} = 0$

$\sin x = \dfrac{\sqrt{3}}{2}$

$x = \pi - \dfrac{\pi}{3}$

$= \dfrac{2\pi}{3}$

π-a | a　Not here since
√S | A　$\frac{\pi}{2} \le x \le \pi$.
π+a | 2π-a
T | C

$a = \sin^{-1}\left(\dfrac{\sqrt{3}}{2}\right)$

$= \dfrac{\pi}{3}$.

Exact value...

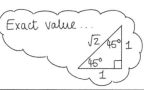

B

7
See **Straight Lines** §3

$m = \tan 135°$
$= -\tan 45°$
$= -1$.

Exact value...

C

8
See **Functions and Graphs** §10

$y = -f(x-2)$ is $y = f(x)$ reflected in the x-axis and then shifted 2 places to the right.

D

9

See **Trigonometry** §3

$\sin a = \dfrac{opp.}{hyp.} = \dfrac{3}{5}$. So we have:

Using Pythagoras's Theorem.

So $\cos a = \dfrac{adj.}{hyp.} = \dfrac{4}{5}$.

Now $\sin(x+a) = \sin x \cos a + \cos x \sin a$
$\qquad\qquad = \dfrac{4}{5}\sin x + \dfrac{3}{5}\cos x$.

B

10

See **Polynomials and Quadratics** §2

The discriminant is $b^2-4ac = 1-4\times1\times1 = 3$.
Since $b^2-4ac < 0$, the roots are <u>not</u> real and <u>not</u> equal.

A

11

See **Vectors** §10

$\overrightarrow{EP} = \underline{p} - \underline{e} = \begin{pmatrix} 1 \\ 5 \\ 7 \end{pmatrix} - \begin{pmatrix} -2 \\ -1 \\ 4 \end{pmatrix} = \begin{pmatrix} 3 \\ 6 \\ 3 \end{pmatrix}$

$\overrightarrow{PF} = \underline{f} - \underline{p} = \begin{pmatrix} 7 \\ 17 \\ 13 \end{pmatrix} - \begin{pmatrix} 1 \\ 5 \\ 7 \end{pmatrix} = \begin{pmatrix} 6 \\ 12 \\ 6 \end{pmatrix} = 2\overrightarrow{EP}$

So $\dfrac{EP}{PF} = \dfrac{1}{2}$, i.e. P divides EF in the ratio $1:2$.

B

2008

12

See **Vectors** §5

From the diagram, $\overrightarrow{VT} = \overrightarrow{VW} + \overrightarrow{WS} + \overrightarrow{ST}$
$$= -\underline{f} - \underline{h} + \underline{g}$$
$$= -\underline{f} + \underline{g} - \underline{h}.$$

C

13

See **Polynomials and Quadratics** §5

Since the parabola crosses the x-axis at 1 and 4, the equation has the form
$$y = k(x-1)(x-4).$$
Since $(0,12)$ lies on the parabola,
$$12 = k \times (-1) \times (-4)$$
$$k = \frac{12}{4}$$
$$= 3.$$
So the equation is $y = 3(x-1)(x-4).$

A

14

See **Further Calculus** §6

$\int 4\sin(2x+3)\,dx = -4 \times \frac{1}{2}\cos(2x+3) + c$
$$= -2\cos(2x+3) + c.$$

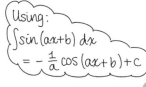

Using:
$\int \sin(ax+b)\,dx$
$= -\frac{1}{a}\cos(ax+b) + c$

B

15

See **Further Calculus** §4

Using the chain rule,

$$\frac{d}{dx}\left(x^3+4\right)^2 = 2\left(x^3+4\right)\times\frac{d}{dx}\left(x^3+4\right)$$

$$= 2\left(x^3+4\right)\times\left(3x^2\right)$$

$$= 6x^2\left(x^3+4\right).$$

C

16

See **Polynomials and Quadratics** §3

Method 1   Compensating...

$$2x^2+4x+7 = 2\left(x^2+2x\right)+7$$
$$= 2\left(x+1\right)^2-2+7 = 2\left(x+1\right)^2+5. \quad \text{So } q=5.$$

This gives the correct x^2 and x terms, and an extra 2.

Take off this extra 2.

Method 2   Comparing coefficients...

$$2x^2+4x+7 = 2\left(x+p\right)^2+q$$
$$= 2x^2+4px+2p^2+q$$

So $4p=4$ and $2p^2+q=7$
      $p=1$ $q=7-2p^2$
                          $=5$

A

2008

17

See **Functions and Graphs** §2

We need $9-x^2 \geqslant 0$
              $x^2 \leqslant 9$
              $-3 \leqslant x \leqslant 3.$

Remember: we can't take the square root of a negative number.

C

18

See **Vectors** §14

$$\underline{q}\cdot(\underline{p}+\underline{q}) = \underline{q}\cdot\underline{p} + \underline{q}\cdot\underline{q}$$
$$= \underline{p}\cdot\underline{q} + |\underline{q}|^2$$
$$= 10 + 4^2$$
$$= 26.$$

Remember:
- $\underline{a}\cdot\underline{b} = \underline{b}\cdot\underline{a}$
- $\underline{a}\cdot\underline{a} = |\underline{a}|^2$

C

19

See **Functions and Graphs** §5

Since $(3,54)$ lies on the curve,
$$54 = 2m^3$$
$$m^3 = 27$$
$$m = \sqrt[3]{27}$$
$$= 3$$

B

20

See **Functions and Graphs** §6

Since $(q, 2)$ lies on the curve,
$$2 = \log_3(q-4)$$
$$q-4 = 3^2$$
$$q = 9+4$$
$$= 13.$$

Remember:
$$y = \log_a x$$
$$\Leftrightarrow x = a^y$$

D

21

(a) See **Differentiation** §7 and §8
(b) See **Polynomials and Quadratics** §9
(c) See **Differentiation** §9

a Stationary points exist where $f'(x) = 0$

$$f'(x) = 3x^2 - 3 = 0$$
$$3x^2 = 3$$
$$x = \pm 1.$$

When $x = -1$, $\quad y = (-1)^3 - 3\times(-1) + 2$
$$= -1 + 3 + 2$$
$$= 4 \qquad (-1,4)$$

When $x = 1$, $\quad y = 1 - 3 + 2 = 0 \qquad (1,0).$

cont...

2008

Method 1 Nature table:

x	-1^-	-1	-1^+	1^-	1	1^+
$f'(x)$	$+$	0	$-$	$-$	0	$+$
Sketch	$/$	$-$	$\setminus$	$\setminus$	$\_$	$/$

Method 2 Second derivative test: $f''(x) = 6x$

$$f''(-1) = -6 < 0 \quad \text{and} \quad f''(1) = 6 > 0.$$

So $(-1, 4)$ is a maximum turning point
$(1, 0)$ is a minimum turning point.

b i **Method 1** From part (a), $f(1) = 0$ (ie $x = 1$ is a root) and so $(x-1)$ is a factor.

Method 2 Using synthetic division...

$$
\begin{array}{r|rrrr}
1 & 1 & 0 & -3 & 2 \\
  &   & 1 & 1 & -2 \\
\hline
  & 1 & 1 & -2 & \boxed{0}
\end{array}
$$

Since the remainder is 0, $x = 1$ is a root so $(x-1)$ is a factor.

ii $x^3 - 3x + 2 = (x-1)(x^2 + x - 2)$ ← (Either by inspection or from
$\qquad\qquad\quad = (x-1)(x-1)(x+2)$ (the bottom row of the table.)

c x-axis (i.e. $y = 0$). From above, $x = -2, 1$.
Hence the curve crosses the x-axis at $(-2, 0)$ and $(1, 0)$.

y-axis (i.e. $x = 0$). $f(0) = 2$
Hence the curve crosses the y-axis at $(0, 2)$.

Using this information, and the stationary points,

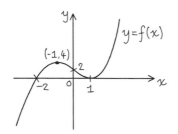

22

(a) See **Differentiation** §5, (b) See **Straight Lines** §6

a
$$\frac{dy}{dx} = 3x^2 - 12x + 8$$

Remember: $\frac{dy}{dx} = m_{tangent}$

So
$$3x^2 - 12x + 8 = -1$$
$$3x^2 - 12x + 9 = 0$$
$$x^2 - 4x + 3 = 0$$
$$(x-1)(x-3) = 0$$
$$x = 1 \quad \text{or} \quad x = 3$$

When $x = 1$, $\quad y = 1 - 6 + 8 = 3$

When $x = 3$, $\quad y = 3^3 - 6 \times 3^2 + 8 \times 3 = 27 - 54 + 24 = -3$.

So the points are $(1,3)$ and $(3,-3)$.

b The line $y = 4 - x$ has gradient -1.
So A must be one of the points found in part (a).

Remember: the line $y = mx + c$ has gradient m.

The equation is only satisfied by $(1,3)$, since $3 = 4 - 1$, and so A is the point $(1,3)$.

23

(a) See **Functions and Graphs** §3
(b) See **Exponentials and Logarithms** §5

a
$$h(f(x)) = h(x^2 - x + 10) = \log_2(x^2 - x + 10).$$
$$h(g(x)) = h(5 - x) = \log_2(5 - x).$$

b
$$\log_2(x^2 - x + 10) - \log_2(5 - x) = 3$$
$$\log_2\left(\frac{x^2 - x + 10}{5 - x}\right) = 3$$
$$\frac{x^2 - x + 10}{5 - x} = 2^3$$
$$x^2 - x + 10 = 40 - 8x$$
$$x^2 + 7x - 30 = 0$$
$$(x + 10)(x - 3) = 0$$
$$x = -10 \quad \text{or} \quad x = 3.$$

Remember:
- $\log_a x - \log_a y = \log_a \frac{x}{y}$
- $\log_a x = y \Leftrightarrow x = a^y$

2008

1

See **Straight Lines** – (a) §9, (b) §7, (c) §10

a $\text{midpoint}_{BC} = \left(\dfrac{-3+5}{2}, \dfrac{-1-5}{2} \right) = (1,-3).$

$m_{BC} = \dfrac{-5-(-1)}{5-(-3)} = -\dfrac{4}{8} = -\dfrac{1}{2}.$ So $m_\perp = 2$ since $m_{BC} \times m_\perp = -1.$

So the equation is
$$y+3 = 2(x-1) \quad \text{using point } (1,-3)$$
$$y+3 = 2x-2$$
$$y = 2x-5$$

b $\text{midpoint}_{AB} = \left(\dfrac{7-3}{2}, \dfrac{9-1}{2} \right) = (2,4).$

$m_{med} = \dfrac{-5-4}{5-2} = \dfrac{-9}{3} = -3.$

So the equation is
$$y+5 = -3(x-5) \quad \text{using } C(5,-5).$$
$$y+5 = -3x+15$$
$$y = -3x+10.$$

c Solve simultaneously...

Method 1 Eliminating y:
$$y = 2x-5 \quad\text{————}\quad ①$$
$$y = -3x+10. \quad\text{————}\quad ②$$
$$①-②: \quad 5x-15=0$$
$$x = 3.$$

Method 2 Equating:
$$2x-5 = -3x+10$$
$$5x = 15$$
$$x = 3.$$

When $x=3$, $y = 2\times3-5 = 1$. So the point of intersection is $(3,1)$

2

See **Vectors** – (a) §7 and §10, (b) §7, (c) §12

a From the diagram, $A(8,0,0)$, $C(0,4,0)$, $E(8,0,6)$ and $G(0,4,6)$.

So $p = a + \frac{2}{3}\overrightarrow{AE} = \begin{pmatrix} 8 \\ 0 \\ 0 \end{pmatrix} + \frac{2}{3}\begin{pmatrix} 0 \\ 0 \\ 6 \end{pmatrix} = \begin{pmatrix} 8 \\ 0 \\ 4 \end{pmatrix}$

$\quad q = c + \frac{1}{2}\overrightarrow{CG} = \begin{pmatrix} 0 \\ 4 \\ 0 \end{pmatrix} + \frac{1}{2}\begin{pmatrix} 0 \\ 0 \\ 6 \end{pmatrix} = \begin{pmatrix} 0 \\ 4 \\ 3 \end{pmatrix}$.

> Note: you don't need to show this working.

Hence $P(8,0,4)$ and $Q(0,4,3)$.

b $\overrightarrow{PQ} = q - p = \begin{pmatrix} 0 \\ 4 \\ 3 \end{pmatrix} - \begin{pmatrix} 8 \\ 0 \\ 4 \end{pmatrix} = \begin{pmatrix} -8 \\ 4 \\ -1 \end{pmatrix}$

$\overrightarrow{PA} = a - p = \begin{pmatrix} 8 \\ 0 \\ 0 \end{pmatrix} - \begin{pmatrix} 8 \\ 0 \\ 4 \end{pmatrix} = \begin{pmatrix} 0 \\ 0 \\ -4 \end{pmatrix}$

> Remember:
> $\overrightarrow{AB} = b - a$.

c $|\overrightarrow{PQ}| = \sqrt{(-8)^2 + 4^2 + (-1)^2} = \sqrt{81} = 9$.

$|\overrightarrow{PA}| = \sqrt{(-4)^2} = 4$

Method 1 $\cos Q\hat{P}A = \dfrac{\overrightarrow{PQ}.\overrightarrow{PA}}{|\overrightarrow{PQ}||\overrightarrow{PA}|}$

> Using:
> $a.b = |a||b|\cos\theta$

$\qquad = \dfrac{-8\times0 + 4\times0 - 1\times(-4)}{9\times4}$

$\qquad = \dfrac{1}{9}$

$Q\hat{P}A = \cos^{-1}\left(\dfrac{1}{9}\right)$

$\qquad = 83\cdot62°$ (to 2 d.p.)

$\qquad$ or $1\cdot459$ rads (to 3 d.p.)

Method 2 $|\overrightarrow{AQ}| = \left|\begin{pmatrix} -8 \\ 4 \\ 3 \end{pmatrix}\right| = \sqrt{89}$.

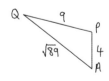

$\cos Q\hat{P}A = \dfrac{81+16-89}{2\times9\times4}$

$\qquad = \dfrac{1}{9}$

> Remember the cosine rule:
> $\cos A = \dfrac{b^2+c^2-a^2}{2bc}$

So $Q\hat{P}A = 83\cdot62°$ (to 2 d.p.) or $1\cdot459$ rads (to 3 d.p.)

3

(a) See **Functions and Graphs** §9 and §10
(b) See **Wave Functions** §2
(c) See **Further Calculus** §1

a i The amplitude is $\sqrt{7}$ so $p = \sqrt{7}$.

ii The amplitude is 3 but the sine graph has also been reflected in the x-axis.

Hence $q = -3$.

b
$$f(x) + g(x) = \sqrt{7}\cos x - 3\sin x$$
$$= k\cos(x+a)$$
$$= k\cos x \cos a - k\sin x \sin a$$
$$= (k\cos a)\cos x - (k\sin a)\sin x$$

Comparing coefficients: $k\sin a = 3$
$k\cos a = \sqrt{7}$

$$\begin{array}{c|c} \checkmark S & A \checkmark\checkmark \\ \hline T & C \checkmark \end{array}$$

So $k = \sqrt{3^2 + \sqrt{7}^2}$ and $\tan a = \dfrac{k\sin a}{k\cos a} = \dfrac{3}{\sqrt{7}}$
$= \sqrt{16}$
$= 4$

$a = \tan^{-1}\left(\dfrac{3}{\sqrt{7}}\right) = 0.848$ (to 3 d.p.)

So $f(x) + g(x) = 4\cos(x + 0.848)$.

c $f'(x) + g'(x) = \dfrac{d}{dx}\big(f(x) + g(x)\big)$

$= \dfrac{d}{dx}\big(4\cos(x+0.848)\big)$ $\left(\text{Using: } \dfrac{d}{dx}\cos x = -\sin x\right)$

$= -4\sin(x + 0.848)$.

4

See **Circles** – (a) §3, (b) §1 and §7, (c) §4

a Comparing with $x^2 + y^2 + 2gx + 2fy + c = 0$,
$2g = 8$, $2f = 4$ and $c = -38$
$g = 4$ $f = 2$.

$\left(\text{The circle } x^2+y^2+2gx+2fy+c=0 \text{ has centre } (-g,-f) \text{ and radius } \sqrt{g^2+f^2-c}\right)$

The centre is $(-4, -2)$.

The radius is $\sqrt{16+4+38} = \sqrt{58}$ units.

cont...

b The circle $(x-4)^2 + (y-6)^2 = 26$ has centre $(4,6)$ and radius $\sqrt{26}$ units.

The distance between the centres is
$$d = \sqrt{(4+4)^2 + (6+2)^2} = \sqrt{128} = 8\sqrt{2} \text{ units.}$$

The sum of the two radii is larger than d since:
$$\sqrt{58} + \sqrt{26} = \underset{>3}{\underline{\sqrt{13}\sqrt{2}}} + \underset{>5}{\underline{\sqrt{29}\sqrt{2}}} > 8\sqrt{2} = d.$$

Since the distance between the centres is less than the sum of the radii, the circles intersect.

c Put $y = 4-x$ in the equation of one of the circles:
$$x^2 + (4-x)^2 + 8x + 4(4-x) - 38 = 0$$
$$x^2 + 16 - 8x + x^2 + 8x + 16 - 4x - 38 = 0$$
$$2x^2 - 4x - 6 = 0$$
$$x^2 - 2x - 3 = 0$$
$$(x+1)(x-3) = 0$$
$$x = -1 \text{ or } x = 3.$$

When $x = -1$, $y = 4 - (-1) = 5$.
When $x = 3$, $y = 4 - 3 = 1$.

So the points of intersection are $(-1, 5)$ and $(3, 1)$.

5

See **Trigonometry** §4 and §5

$$\cos 2x° + 2\sin x° = \sin^2 x°$$
$$1 - 2\sin^2 x° + 2\sin x° = \sin^2 x°$$
$$3\sin^2 x° - 2\sin x° - 1 = 0$$
$$(3\sin x° + 1)(\sin x° - 1) = 0$$

Using:
$$\cos 2A = 1 - 2\sin^2 A$$

$3\sin x° + 1 = 0$
$\sin x° = -\frac{1}{3}$

$$\begin{array}{c|c} 180-a & a \\ S & A \\ \hline \sqrt{T} & C \checkmark \\ 180+a & 360-a \end{array}$$

or $\quad \sin x° - 1 = 0$
$\sin x° = 1$
$x = 90$

$$a = \sin^{-1}\left(\frac{1}{3}\right)$$
$$= 19.47 \text{ (to 2 d.p.)}$$

$x = 180 + 19.47$ or $360 - 19.47$ or 90
$\quad = 199.47 \quad$ or $\quad 340.53 \quad$ or 90

6

(a) See **Straight Lines** §6
(b) See **Polynomials and Quadratics** §4 or **Differentiation** §12

a The line has gradient −2 and y-axis intercept 6.
So its equation is $y = -2x + 6$.

The length QR is the y-coordinate of the point on this line with x-coordinate t, i.e.

$$QR = -2t + 6 = 6 - 2t.$$

b The area of the rectangle is given by $A = \text{length} \times \text{breadth}$
$$= t(6 - 2t).$$

Method 1   Sketch $A = t(6 - 2t)$.

Crosses t-axis when $t(6 - 2t) = 0$
$$t = 0 \text{ or } 6 - 2t = 0$$
$$t = 3$$

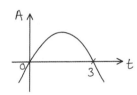

The parabola is concave down (∩-shaped) because the coefficient of t^2 is negative.

The maximum lies mid-way between the roots, ie when $t = \frac{3}{2}$.

Method 2 $A = 6t - 2t^2$.
Stationary points exist where $\frac{dA}{dt} = 0$.

$$\frac{dA}{dt} = 6 - 4t = 0$$
$$4t = 6$$
$$t = \frac{3}{2}$$

Nature:

t	$\frac{3}{2}^-$	$\frac{3}{2}$	$\frac{3}{2}^+$
$\frac{dA}{dt}$	+	0	−
Sketch	/	—	\

OR $\frac{d^2A}{dt^2} = -4$

Hence $t = \frac{3}{2}$ gives the maximum area.

When $t = \frac{3}{2}$, $QR = 6 - 2 \times \frac{3}{2} = 3$.

Hence Q is $\left(\frac{3}{2}, 3\right)$.

7

See **Integration** §7 or §6

First notice that the shaded area is symmetrical about the y-axis. So first calculate the area for $x > 0$, then double.

Method 1 Rearrange for x and integrate with respect to y.

$$y = 32 - 2x^2$$
$$2x^2 = 32 - y$$
$$x = \left(16 - \frac{y}{2}\right)^{1/2} \quad \text{(Only consider } x > 0.\text{)}$$

So half the shaded area is given by

$$\int_{14}^{24} \left(16 - \frac{1}{2}y\right)^{1/2} dy = \left[\frac{\left(16 - \frac{y}{2}\right)^{3/2}}{\frac{3}{2} \times \left(-\frac{1}{2}\right)}\right]_{14}^{24}$$

Remember:
$$\int (ax+b)^n dx$$
$$= \frac{(ax+b)^{n+1}}{a(n+1)} + c$$

$$= \left[-\frac{4}{3}\sqrt{16 - \frac{y}{2}}^3\right]_{14}^{24}$$

$$= -\frac{4}{3}\sqrt{4}^3 + \frac{4}{3}\sqrt{9}^3$$

$$= \frac{76}{3} \quad \left(= 25\frac{1}{3}\right)$$

Hence the shaded area is $\frac{152}{3}$ $\left(\text{or } 50\frac{2}{3}\right)$ square units.

cont...

Method 2

Find a and b.

a: $32 - 2x^2 = 24$
$\qquad 2x^2 = 8$
$\qquad\ \ x = 2$

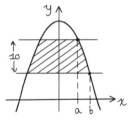

Only consider $x > 0$.

i.e. $a = 2$.

b: $32 - 2x^2 = 14$
$\qquad 2x^2 = 18$
$\qquad\ x = 3$.

i.e. $b = 3$.

The shaded area between a and b is given by

$$\int_2^3 (\text{upper} - \text{lower})\, dx$$

$$= \int_2^3 (32 - 2x^2 - 14)\, dx$$

$$= \left[18x - \frac{2}{3}x^3 \right]_2^3$$

$$= 54 - \frac{2}{3} \times 27 - 36 + \frac{2}{3} \times 8$$

$$= \frac{16}{3} \quad \left(= 5\frac{1}{3} \right)$$

So the total shaded area is

$$2 \left(10 \times 2 + \frac{16}{3} \right) = \frac{152}{3} \quad \text{or} \quad 50\frac{2}{3} \quad \text{square units.}$$

1   *See **Sequences** §2*

$u_2 = 3u_1 + 4 = 3 \times 2 + 4 = 10.$
$u_3 = 3u_2 + 4 = 3 \times 10 + 4 = 34.$

A

2   *See **Circles** §3*

Comparing with $x^2 + y^2 + 2gx + 2fy + c$,

$2g = 8$, $2f = 6$ and $c = -75$
$g = 4$ $f = 3$

The circle
$x^2 + y^2 + 2gx + 2fy + c = 0$
has radius $\sqrt{g^2 + f^2 - c}$.

The radius is $\sqrt{4^2 + 3^2 + 75} = \sqrt{16 + 9 + 75} = \sqrt{100} = 10.$

B

3   *See **Straight Lines** §7*

$S = \text{midpoint}_{QR} = \left(\frac{3-1}{2}, \frac{6-(-4)}{2} \right) = (1, 5).$

So $m_{PS} = \frac{5 - (-2)}{1 - (-3)} = \frac{7}{4}.$

D

4   *See **Differentiation** §5*

$\frac{dy}{dx} = 15x^2 - 12.$

Remember: the derivative gives the gradient of the tangent.

When $x = 1$, the gradient of the tangent is $15 \times 1^2 - 12 = 3$

C

5   *See **Straight Lines** §1 and §3*

The length of ST is $\sqrt{(5-2)^2 + (-1-3)^2} = \sqrt{3^2 + 4^2} = 5$ units

$m_{ST} = \frac{-1-3}{5-2} = -\frac{4}{3}.$

B

6

See **Sequences** §4

__Method 1__ $l = \dfrac{b}{1-a}$ with $a = 0.7$ and $b = 10$.

$l = \dfrac{10}{1-0.7} = \dfrac{10}{0.3} = \dfrac{100}{3}$.

__Method 2__   As $n \to \infty$, $u_{n+1} = u_n = l$

So $l = 0.7l + 10$

$0.3l = 10$

$l = \dfrac{10}{0.3} = \dfrac{100}{3}$.

A

7

See **Trigonometry** §4

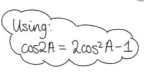

$\begin{aligned}
\cos 2x &= 2\cos^2 x - 1 \\
&= 2\left(\dfrac{1}{\sqrt{5}}\right)^2 - 1 \\
&= \dfrac{2}{5} - 1 \\
&= -\dfrac{3}{5}.
\end{aligned}$

Using:
$\cos 2A = 2\cos^2 A - 1$

A

8

See **Differentiation** §2

$\dfrac{1}{4x^3} = \dfrac{1}{4}x^{-3}$.

So $\dfrac{d}{dx}\left(\dfrac{1}{4x^3}\right) = \dfrac{d}{dx}\left(\dfrac{1}{4}x^{-3}\right) = -\dfrac{3}{4}x^{-4} = -\dfrac{3}{4x^4}$.

D

9

See **Circles** §4

Put $y = 2x$ in the equation of the circle:

$\begin{aligned}
x^2 + (2x)^2 &= 5 \\
x^2 + 4x^2 &= 5 \\
5x^2 &= 5 \\
x^2 &= 1 \\
x &= \pm 1.
\end{aligned}$

A

10

See **Functions and Graphs** §6 and §10 or **Exponentials and Logarithms** §7

<u>Method 1</u>   The curve $y = \log_5 x$ has graph

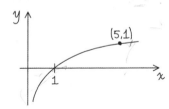

and $y = \log_5 (x-2)$ is this shifted 2 units to the right.

<u>Method 2</u>   When $y = 0$, $\log_5 (x-2) = 0$
$$x - 2 = 5^0$$
$$x = 3.$$

So the curve passes through $(3,0)$.

B

11

See **Trigonometry** §1

$(4\sin x - \sqrt{5})(\sin x + 1) = 0$

$4\sin x - \sqrt{5} = 0$ or $\sin x + 1 = 0$

$\sin x = \dfrac{\sqrt{5}}{4}$ $\sin x = -1$

$y = \sin x$

One solution

Since $\dfrac{\sqrt{5}}{4} < 1$ thus part has two solutions in $0 \le x < 2\pi$,

Therefore there are 3 solutions in $0 \le x < 2\pi$.

B

12

See **Polynomials and Quadratics** §2

Let $a = 2$, $b = -1$ and $c = -9$, then the discriminant is
$$b^2 - 4ac = (-1)^2 - 4 \times 2 \times (-9) = 1 + 72 = 73.$$

Since $b^2 - 4ac > 0$, the roots are real and distinct, and because 73 is not a square number, the roots are not rational.

C

2009

13

See **Wave Functions** §1

$k\sin a° = 1$
$k\cos a° = \sqrt{3}$

$\begin{array}{c|c} \text{S} & \text{A} \checkmark\checkmark \\ \hline \text{T} & \text{C} \checkmark \end{array}$

So $k = \sqrt{1^2 + \sqrt{3}^2}$ and $\tan a° = \dfrac{k\sin a°}{k\cos a°} = \dfrac{1}{\sqrt{3}}$
$\quad\quad = \sqrt{4}$
$\quad\quad = 2$
$\quad\quad\quad\quad\quad\quad\quad\quad a = \tan^{-1}\left(\dfrac{1}{\sqrt{3}}\right)$
$\quad\quad\quad\quad\quad\quad\quad\quad\quad\quad = 30.$

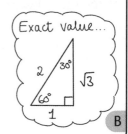

Exact value...

B

14

See **Functions and Graphs** §9 and §10

$f(x) = 2\sin\left(3x - \dfrac{\pi}{2}\right) + 5$

Scales the graph to have amplitude 2

Shifts the graph 5 units up the y-axis.

So the range is $3 \le f(x) \le 7$.

C

15

See **Straight Lines** §3

The line makes an angle of $\dfrac{\pi}{2} - \dfrac{\pi}{6} = \dfrac{\pi}{3}$ with the positive direction of the x-axis.

So the gradient is $\tan\dfrac{\pi}{3} = \sqrt{3}$.

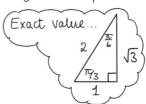

Exact value...

A

16

See **Integration** §5

Since the shaded region lies below the x-axis, its area is given by

$$-\int_0^1 (4x^3 - 9x^2)\,dx = -\left[x^4 - 3x^3\right]_0^1.$$

B

17 See **Vectors** §3

$|\underline{u}| = \sqrt{(-3)^2 + 4^2} = \sqrt{25} = 5.$

So $\frac{1}{5}\underline{u}$ is a unit vector parallel to $\underline{u}$.

$\frac{1}{5}\underline{u} = \begin{pmatrix} -3/5 \\ 0 \\ 4/5 \end{pmatrix} = -\frac{3}{5}\underline{i} + \frac{4}{5}\underline{k}.$

A

18 See **Further Calculus** §4

Using the chain rule,

$$f'(x) = -\frac{1}{2}(4-3x^2)^{-3/2} \times \frac{d}{dx}(4-3x^2)$$
$$= -\frac{1}{2}(4-3x^2)^{-3/2} \times (-6x)$$
$$= 3x(4-3x^2)^{-3/2}.$$

D

19 See **Polynomials and Quadratics** §6

$6 + x - x^2 < 0$

$-(x^2 - x - 6) < 0$

$-(x+2)(x-3) < 0$

From the sketch, $x < -2$ or $x > 3$.

Sketch:

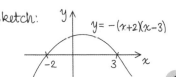

$y = -(x+2)(x-3)$

C

20 See **Differentiation** §4

$\frac{dA}{dr} = 4\pi r + 6\pi.$

When $r = 2$, $\frac{dA}{dr} = 8\pi + 6\pi = 14\pi.$

Remember: "rate of change" means "derivative".

C

2009

91

21

See **Straight Lines** – (a) §6, (b) §8, (c) §6 and §10

a Put $y = 0$ in the equation of PQ:

$$6x - 7 \times 0 + 18 = 0$$
$$6x = -18$$
$$x = -3. \quad \text{So P has coordinates } (-3, 0).$$

b $m_{QR} = \dfrac{-2-6}{8-4} = \dfrac{-8}{4} = -2.$ So $m_{alt.} = \dfrac{1}{2}$ since $m_{QR} \times m_{alt.} = -1.$

So the equation is $\quad y = \dfrac{1}{2}(x+3) \quad$ using point $P(-3,0)$

$$2y = x + 3$$

c We know $m_{QR} = -2.$

So the equation of QR is $\quad y - 6 = -2(x-4) \quad$ using point $Q(4,6).$
$$y - 6 = -2x + 8$$
$$y = -2x + 14.$$

Solve the equations of QR and PT simultaneously...

$$2y = x + 3 \quad \text{———} \quad ①$$
$$y = -2x + 14 \quad \text{———} \quad ②$$

$② + 2 \times ①: \quad 5y = 20$
$$\qquad\qquad y = 4$$

When $y = 4$, $\quad x = 2 \times 4 - 3 = 5.$ So T is the point $(5,4).$

22 See **Vectors** – (a) §9 and §10, (b) §13

a **i** $\overrightarrow{DE} = \underline{e} - \underline{d} = \begin{pmatrix} 1 \\ -2 \\ -3 \end{pmatrix} - \begin{pmatrix} 10 \\ -8 \\ -15 \end{pmatrix} = \begin{pmatrix} -9 \\ 6 \\ 12 \end{pmatrix} = 3\begin{pmatrix} -3 \\ 2 \\ 4 \end{pmatrix}$

$\overrightarrow{EF} = \underline{f} - \underline{e} = \begin{pmatrix} -2 \\ 0 \\ 1 \end{pmatrix} - \begin{pmatrix} 1 \\ -2 \\ -3 \end{pmatrix} = \begin{pmatrix} -3 \\ 2 \\ 4 \end{pmatrix}$

$\overrightarrow{EF}$ and $\overrightarrow{DE}$ have a common point and, since $3\overrightarrow{EF} = \overrightarrow{DE}$, they have a common direction. Hence D, E and F are collinear.

ii Since $3\overrightarrow{EF} = \overrightarrow{DE}$, E divides DF in the ratio $3:1$.

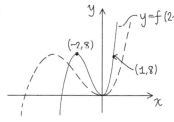

b $\overrightarrow{GE} = \underline{e} - \underline{g} = \begin{pmatrix} 1 \\ -2 \\ -3 \end{pmatrix} - \begin{pmatrix} k \\ 1 \\ 0 \end{pmatrix} = \begin{pmatrix} 1-k \\ -3 \\ -3 \end{pmatrix}$.

Since DE and GE are perpendicular, $\overrightarrow{DE}.\overrightarrow{GE} = 0$. So

$$-9(1-k) + 6 \times (-3) + 12 \times (-3) = 0$$
$$-9 + 9k - 18 - 36 = 0$$
$$9k = 63$$
$$k = 7.$$

23 See **Functions and Graphs** §10

a

$y = f(2x)$ multiplies each x-coordinate by $\frac{1}{2}$.

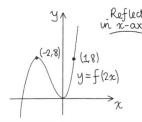

b $y = 1 - f(2x) = -f(2x) + 1$.

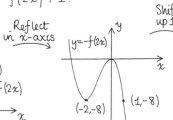 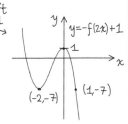

24

See **Trigonometry** §3

a $\sin\left(\frac{7\pi}{12}\right) = \sin\left(\frac{\pi}{3} + \frac{\pi}{4}\right) = \sin\frac{\pi}{3}\cos\frac{\pi}{4} + \cos\frac{\pi}{3}\sin\frac{\pi}{4}$

$$= \frac{\sqrt{3}}{2} \times \frac{1}{\sqrt{2}} + \frac{1}{2} \times \frac{1}{\sqrt{2}}$$

$$= \frac{\sqrt{3}+1}{2\sqrt{2}}$$

Using:
$\sin(A+B)$
$= \sin A\cos B + \cos A\sin B$

b $\sin(A+B) = \sin A\cos B + \cos A\sin B$

$\sin(A-B) = \sin A\cos B - \cos A\sin B$

Adding gives $\sin(A+B) + \sin(A-B) = 2\sin A\cos B$.

c i $\frac{\pi}{12} = \frac{\pi}{3} - \frac{\pi}{4}$

ii Since $\frac{7\pi}{12} = \frac{\pi}{3} + \frac{\pi}{4}$ and $\frac{\pi}{12} = \frac{\pi}{3} - \frac{\pi}{4}$, use the above formula

with $A = \frac{\pi}{3}$ and $B = \frac{\pi}{4}$.

$$\sin\left(\frac{7\pi}{12}\right) + \sin\left(\frac{\pi}{12}\right) = 2\sin\frac{\pi}{3}\cos\frac{\pi}{4}$$

$$= 2 \times \frac{\sqrt{3}}{2} \times \frac{1}{\sqrt{2}}$$

$$= \frac{\sqrt{3}}{\sqrt{2}} = \frac{\sqrt{6}}{2}$$

Exact values...

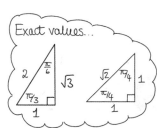

1

*See **Differentiation** §7 and §8*

Stationary points exist where $\frac{dy}{dx} = 0$.

$$\frac{dy}{dx} = 3x^2 - 6x - 9 = 0$$
$$3(x^2 - 2x - 3) = 0$$
$$(x+1)(x-3) = 0$$
$$x = -1, \quad x = 3.$$

When $x = -1$,
$$y = (-1)^3 - 3 \times (-1)^2 - 9 \times (-1) + 12$$
$$= -1 - 3 + 9 + 12$$
$$= 17. \qquad (-1, 17)$$

When $x = 3$,
$$y = 3^3 - 3 \times 3^2 - 9 \times 3 + 12$$
$$= -15. \qquad (3, -15).$$

Method 1 Nature table:

x	-1^{-}	-1	-1^{+}	3^{-}	3	3^{+}
dy/dx	$+$	0	$-$	$-$	0	$+$
Sketch	/	—	\	\	_	/

Method 2 Second derivative test: $\quad \frac{d^2y}{dx^2} = 6x - 6$.

When $x = -1$, $\frac{d^2y}{dx^2} = 6 \times (-1) - 6 = -12 < 0$

When $x = 3$, $\frac{d^2y}{dx^2} = 6 \times 3 - 6 = 12 > 0$.

So $(-1, 17)$ is a maximum turning point.
$(3, -15)$ is a minimum turning point.

2

(a) See **Functions and Graphs** §3
(b) See **Differentiation** §2

a **i** $p(x) = f(g(x)) = f(x^2-2) = 3(x^2-2)+1 = 3x^2-5.$

ii $q(x) = g(f(x)) = g(3x+1) = (3x+1)^2-2.$

b $p'(x) = 6x$ and $q'(x) = 2(3x+1) \times \dfrac{d}{dx}(3x+1) = 6(3x+1).$

So $6x = 6(3x+1)$

$\quad x = 3x+1$

$\quad 2x = -1$

$\quad x = -\dfrac{1}{2}.$

3

(a) See **Polynomials and Quadratics** §9
(b) See **Exponentials and Logarithms** §3 and §5

a **i** <u>Method 1</u> Put $x=1$ in the left-hand side:

$1^3 + 8 \times 1^2 + 11 \times 1 - 20 = 1 + 8 + 11 - 20 = 0.$

So $x = 1$ is a root of the equation.

<u>Method 2</u> Using synthetic division...

$$
\begin{array}{r|rrrr}
1 & 1 & 8 & 11 & -20 \\
  &   & 1 & 9 & 20 \\
\hline
  & 1 & 9 & 20 & 0
\end{array}
$$

Since the remainder is 0, $x = 1$ is a root.

ii $x^3 + 8x^2 + 11x - 20 = (x-1)(x^2 + 9x + 20)$ ← By inspection or from the table.

$\qquad\qquad\qquad\qquad\quad = (x-1)(x+4)(x+5).$

cont...

b $\log_2(x+3) + \log_2(x^2+5x-4) = 3$

$\log_2\left((x+3)(x^2+5x-4)\right) = 3$

$(x+3)(x^2+5x-4) = 2^3$

$x^3 + 8x^2 + 11x - 12 = 8$

$x^3 + 8x^2 + 11x - 20 = 0$

$(x-1)(x+4)(x+5) = 0$

So $x = 1$, $x = -4$, $x = -5$

> Remember:
> • $\log_a x + \log_a y = \log_a xy$
> • $\log_a x = y \Leftrightarrow x = a^y$

> Remember: we can only take log of a positive number.

But when $x = -4$, $\log_2(x+3) = \log_2(-1)$ which is undefined.

$x = -5$, $\log_2(x+3) = \log_2(-2)$ which is undefined.

So the only solution is $x = 1$.

4

(a) See **Circles** §2
(b) See **Straight Lines** §2 and **Circles** §6
(c) See **Circles** §7

a Put $x = 5$ and $y = 10$ in the left-hand side:

$(5+1)^2 + (10-2)^2 = 36 + 64 = 100$.

Since this equals the right-hand side, P lies on the circle.

b The circle has centre $C(-1, 2)$.

> The circle $(x-a)^2 + (y-b)^2 = r^2$ has centre (a, b).

Let Q have coordinates (x_Q, y_Q). Since C is the midpoint of PQ,

$(-1, 2) = \left(\dfrac{x_Q+5}{2}, \dfrac{y_Q+10}{2}\right)$.

So $x_Q + 5 = -2$ and $y_Q + 10 = 4$

$x_Q = -7$ $\qquad y_Q = -6$.

Hence Q is the point $(-7, -6)$.

Now $m_{PQ} = m_{CP} = \dfrac{10-2}{5-(-1)} = \dfrac{8}{6} = \dfrac{4}{3}$,

so $m_{tgt} = -\dfrac{3}{4}$ since $m_{PQ} \times m_{tgt} = -1$.

cont...

Therefore the equation of the tangent at Q is

$$y + 6 = -\frac{3}{4}(x+7) \quad \text{using } Q(-7,-6).$$
$$4y + 24 = -3x - 21$$
$$3x + 4y + 45 = 0.$$

c Circle C_1 has radius 10.
So the radii of C_2 and C_3 are both 20.

> The circle $(x-a)^2 + (y-b)^2 = r^2$ has radius r.

The point $P(5,10)$ is the centre of C_2, so the equation of C_2 is

Sketch:

$$(x-5)^2 + (y-10)^2 = 20^2$$
i.e. $(x-5)^2 + (y-10)^2 = 400.$

The point Q is the midpoint of PR, so

$$\left(\frac{5+x_R}{2}, \frac{10+y_R}{2}\right) = (-7,-6)$$

i.e. $\dfrac{5+x_R}{2} = -7$ and $\dfrac{10+y_R}{2} = -6$

$$x_R = -19. \qquad\qquad y_R = -22.$$

So R is the point $(-19,-22)$ and C_3 has equation

$$(x+19)^2 + (y+22)^2 = 400.$$

5

(a) See **Functions and Graphs** §9 and §10
(b) See **Trigonometry** §1
(c) See **Integration** §6

a The period of $g(x)$ is π, so $n=2$. The amplitude is 3 so $m=3$.

b The curves intersect where

$$-4\cos2x + 3 = 3\cos2x$$
$$7\cos2x = 3$$
$$\cos2x = \frac{3}{7}.$$

$$\begin{array}{c|c} \pi-a & a \\ \hline S & A \;\checkmark \\ \hline T & C \;\checkmark \\ \hline \pi+a & 2\pi-a \end{array}$$

$$a = \cos^{-1}\left(\frac{3}{7}\right)$$
$$= 1.128 \quad (\text{to } 3 \text{ d.p.})$$

So $2x = 1.128$ or $2x = 2\pi - 1.128$
$\quad x = 0.564 \qquad x = 2.578 \; (\text{to } 3 \text{ d.p.})$

> To get a more accurate answer, we can work to 3 d.p. and round at the end.

When $x = 0.564$, $y = 3\cos(2 \times 0.564)$
$\qquad\qquad\qquad = 1.285.$

When $x = 2.578$, $y = 3\cos(2 \times 2.578)$
$\qquad\qquad\qquad = 1.288.$ (both to 3 d.p.)

So the points of intersection are $(0.6, 1.3)$ and $(2.6, 1.3)$ to 1 d.p.

c The shaded area is

$$\int_{0.6}^{2.6} (\text{upper} - \text{lower}) \, dx$$

$$= \int_{0.6}^{2.6} \left(-4\cos2x + 3 - 3\cos2x\right) dx$$

$$= \int_{0.6}^{2.6} \left(-7\cos2x + 3\right) dx$$

$$= \left[-\frac{7}{2}\sin2x + 3x\right]_{0.6}^{2.6}$$

> Using:
> $\int \cos ax \, dx = \frac{1}{a}\sin ax + c$

$$= 10.89 + 1.46$$
$$= 12.4 \quad \text{square units} \; (\text{to } 1 \text{ d.p.})$$

6

See *Exponentials and Logarithms* §5

a Let N be the population in millions.

- The rate of increase is $1.6\% = 0.016$. So $r = 0.016$.
- 2020 is 14 years after 2006, so $t = 14$.

$N = N_0 e^{rt} = 61 e^{0.016 \times 14} = 76.32$ (to 2 d.p.)

So the population would be 76.32 million.

b This time, $r = 0.43\% = 0.0043$.

For the population to double, $N = 2N_0$ so

$$N = N_0 e^{0.0043t}$$
$$2N_0 = N_0 e^{0.0043t}$$
$$e^{0.0043t} = 2$$
$$0.0043t = \log_e 2$$

Remember:
$$a^y = x \Leftrightarrow y = \log_a x$$

$$t = \frac{\log_e 2}{0.0043}$$

$$t = 161.20 \text{ (to 2 d.p.)}$$

So the population would take 161.20 years to double.

7

See **Vectors** – (a) §14 and §11, (b) §5 and §3

a

$$\underline{p} \cdot (\underline{q} + \underline{r}) = \underline{p} \cdot \underline{q} + \underline{p} \cdot \underline{r}$$

$$= |\underline{p}||\underline{q}| \cos 30° + 0 \quad \longleftarrow \text{ since } \underline{p} \text{ and } \underline{r} \text{ are perpendicular.}$$

$$= 4 \times 3 \times \cos 30°$$

$$= 4 \times 3 \times \frac{\sqrt{3}}{2}$$

$$= 6\sqrt{3}.$$

Exact values...

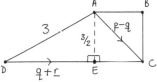

$$\underline{r} \cdot (\underline{p} - \underline{q}) = \underline{r} \cdot \underline{p} - \underline{r} \cdot \underline{q}$$

$$= 0 - |\underline{r}||\underline{q}| \cos\theta$$

$$= -\frac{3}{2} \times 3 \times (-\cos 60°)$$

$$= \frac{3}{2} \times 3 \times \frac{1}{2}$$

$$= \frac{9}{4}.$$

$\theta = 60°$

$|\underline{r}| = 3\sin 30° = \frac{3}{2}$.

b From the diagram, $\underline{q} + \underline{r} = \overrightarrow{DE}$
and $\underline{p} - \underline{q} = -\underline{q} + \underline{p} = \overrightarrow{AC}$.

Using Pythagoras's theorem:

$$|\underline{q} + \underline{r}| = \sqrt{3^2 - \left(\tfrac{3}{2}\right)^2} = \sqrt{\frac{27}{4}} = \frac{\sqrt{9}\sqrt{3}}{\sqrt{4}} = \frac{3\sqrt{3}}{2} \quad \left(= 2 \cdot 60 \text{ to } 2 \text{ d.p.}\right)$$

Now $|EC| = |\underline{p}| - \frac{3\sqrt{3}}{2} = 4 - \frac{3\sqrt{3}}{2}$

So $|\underline{p} - \underline{q}| = \sqrt{\left(4 - \frac{3\sqrt{3}}{2}\right)^2 + \left(\frac{3}{2}\right)^2} = \sqrt{25 - 12\sqrt{3}} \quad \left(= 2 \cdot 05 \text{ to } 2 \text{ d.p.}\right)$